distortions clicks & pops
from analog equipment
are part of the fabric
& only contribute
to the garment's uniqueness
& sound quality

ALSO BY KEVIN YOUNG

Most Way Home

*Giant Steps: The New Generation of African
American Writers* (Editor)

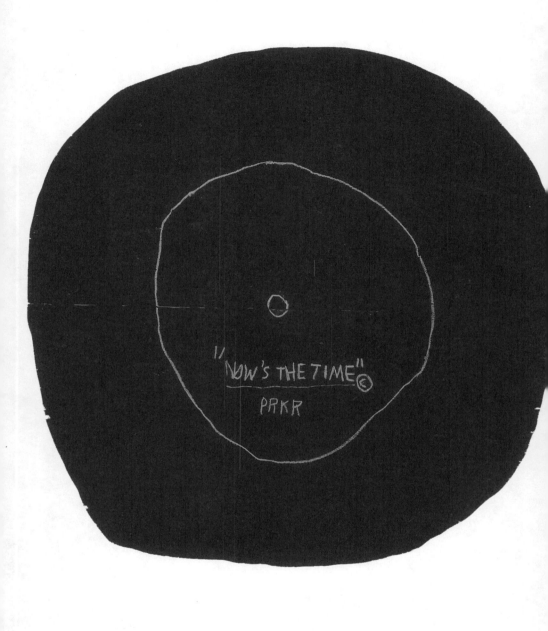

To Repel Ghosts

five sides in B minor

{ sung by the author }

Kevin Young

Z

ZOLAND BOOKS
Cambridge, Massachusetts

First edition published in 2001 by
Zoland Books, Inc.
384 Huron Avenue
Cambridge, Massachusetts 02138

FIRST EDITION

Book design by Janis Owens

Frontispiece, *Now's the Time* by Jean-Michel Basquiat.
© 2001 Artists Rights Society (ARS), New York / ADAGP, Paris.
Courtesy The Brant Foundation, Greenwich, CT.
Cover, *To Repel Ghosts* by Jean-Michel Basquiat © 2000 Artists Rights
Society (ARS) New York/ADAGP, Paris

Printed in the United States of America

05 04 03 02 01   8 7 6 5 4 3 2 1

This book is printed on acid-free paper, and its binding materials have
been chosen for strength and durability.

Library of Congress Cataloging-in-Publication Data
Young, Kevin.
To repel ghosts / Kevin Young.
p. cm.
ISBN 1-58195-033-0
1. Basquiat, Jean-Michel—Poetry. 2. Artists—Poetry. I. Title

PS3575.O798 T6 2001
811'.54—dc21
00-067311

Contents

DISC 2: MOJO

SIDE 4: B-SIDES

There is that great proverb, that until the lions have their own historians, the history of the hunt will always glorify the hunter. That did not come to me until much later. Once I realized that, I had to be a writer. I had to be that historian. It's not one man's job. It's not one person's job. But it is something we have to do, so that the story of the hunt will also reflect the agony, the travail, the bravery, even, of the lions.

—CHINUA ACHEBE

Hide and write and study and think. I know what factions do. Beware of them. I know what lionizers do. Beware of them.

—VACHEL LINDSAY TO LANGSTON HUGHES

> Why Lion, you look like to me
> You been in the precinct station
> And had the third-degree
> Else you look like
> You been high on gage
> And done got caught
> In a monkey cage!
> You ain't no king to me.

—TRADITIONAL

Prehistory

INDIA (CONT.)

DRAGON SWALLOWS WATERS OF EARTH
EARLY CIVILIZATION————
FIRE MYTHS

FOUR AGES OF THE WORLD, DOCTRINE
GODS (GREAT MOTHER©————
HEAT AND COLD IN MYTHS

HEAVENS, STRUCTURE OF
LITERATURE
MAP

SERPENTS, MYTHS, ~~HERO~~——
SMITHS AS HEROES
SNAKE GOD COUPLE

SOLAR WHEEL
SOMA, DRINK OF THE GODS
SPIRITS

STUPAS
SUN GODS + SYMBOLS
WAR GOD

INDIANS (AMERICAN)

ANIMALS IN THE SKY

ASIATIC ORIGIN OF
BUFFALO MYTHS
CATASTROPHE MYTHS

CLIFFHOUSE
COLOR SYMBOLISM
CREATION OF MAN

CREATION OF WORLD
FIRE BRINGERS
GREAT SPIRIT

HARE AS GOD
MEDICINE MEN
MOON MYTHS

VIRGIN BIRTH OF HEROS

Side **1** Bootlegs

1. CAMPBELL'S BLACK BEAN SOUP.
2. · POISON OASIS. 1981.
3. CADILLAC MOON. 1981.
4. SPACE PORK. 1977.
5. CITY-AS-SCHOOL.
6. VOCABULARIO.
7. BROTHERS SAUSAGE. 1983.
8. MAN-MADE.
9. CANAL ZONE. 1979.
10. GRINGO PILOT. 1981.
11. 3 KINDS OF FENCES.
12. MONARCHS.
13. OLEO.
14. GRAY.
15. NEW YORK/NEW WAVE.

16. NEW YORK BEAT. 1980-81.
17. TIMES SQUARE SHOW.
18. BEYOND WORDS.
19. DEFACEMENT. 1983.
20. SIX CRIMEE.
21. IRONY OF NEGRO POLICEMAN. 1981.
22. OBNOXIOUS LIBERALS. 1982.
23. DOS CABEZAS. 1982.
24. AMATEUR BOUT.
25. OXIDATION PORTRAIT OF JEAN-MICHEL BASQUIAT. 1982.
26. DIMENSIONS.
27. VNDRZ. 1982.

DISC **1** : ZYDECO

{ Portrait of the Artist as a Young Derelict }

PAY FOR SOUP
BUILD A FORT
SET THAT ON FIRE

—UNTITLED, 1981

1. Campbell's Black Bean Soup

Candid, Warhol
scoffed, coined it
a nigger's loft—

not The Factory,
Basquiat's studio stood
anything but lofty—

skid rows of canvases,
paint peeling like bananas,
scabs. Bartering work

for horse, Basquiat churned
out butter, signing each
SAMO©. Sameold. Sambo's

soup. How to sell out
something bankrupt
already? How to copy

rights? Basquiat stripped
labels, opened & ate
alphabets, chicken

& noodle. Not even brown
broth left beneath, not one
black bean, he smacked

the very bottom, scraping
the uncanny, making
a tin thing sing.

2. Poison Oasis   { 1981 }

Such church hurts—
all haloes, crowns,
coins ancient,

flattened. Cross-
roads. Money changes
hands stained

like glass. Mirror,
mirage—the dog
a praying mantis at his

feet. Basquiat eyes
the needle, needs
a fix—if the camel fits—

heaven. *Gimme*
some smack
or I'll smack

you back. Which side
should he pierce,
where to place

the dromedary
in his vein? Each opening
fills with wine

a wound. Hollowed
ground. Blood
of our blood—

Basquiat trades
Golgotha, skulls
& all, for an armful

of stigmata.
Runs a game,
plays snakes

& ladders, shooting
up. SAMO says: IF SOMEONE
SMITES YOU, TURN

THE OTHER FACE.
Even falling
has its grace—injection

& genuflection
both bring you
to your knees,

make you prey.

6

3. Cadillac Moon   { 1981 }

Crashing
again—Basquiat
sends fenders

& letters headlong
into each other,
the future. Fusion.

AAAAAAAAAAA.

Big Bang. The Big
Apple, Atom's,
behind him—

no sirens
in sight. His career
of careening

since—at six—
playing stickball
a car stole

his spleen. Blind
sided. Move
along folks—nothing

to see here. Driven,
does two Caddys
colliding, biting

the dust he's begun
to snort. Hit
& run. Red

Cross—the pill-pale
ambulance, inside
out, he hitched

to the hospital.
Joy ride. Hot
wired. O the rush

before the wreck—

each Cadillac
a Titanic,
an iceberg that's met

its match—cabin
flooded
like an engine,

drawing even
dark Shine
from below deck.

FLATS FIX. Chop

shop. Body work
while-u-wait. *In situ
the spleen*

or lien, anterior view—
removed. Given
Gray's Anatomy

by his mother for recovery—

*151. Reflexion of spleen
turned forwards
& to the right, like*

pages of a book—
Basquiat pulled
into orbit

with tide, the moon
gold as a tooth,
a hubcap gleaming,

gleaned—Shine
swimming for land,
somewhere solid

to spin his own obit.

4. Space Pork   { 1977 }

1.
Spaced out, a ship

2.
POLICE—
PUT OUT THAT "J"
Comic stripped

YAAAAAA!

3.
THEY CAN SMOKE
THAT CONGO DUST
SOMEPLACE ELSE

says the talking pig—
star on his helmet
face fat as bacon

4.
LATER THAT NIGHT
OFFICER HARDON
WAS IN

THE MOOD
FOR A HASSLE...
LET ME SEE

YOUR READ-OUT SHEET

Leave me alone
answers the man on
horizon to copship above

6.
I SAID...GRUNT

Very well—
Sic'm

9.
K R U N C H
Yea Baby
Eat those cops...

3.

CHOMP CHEW
SMEK
C'mon babe

Let's go home
& fry
some bird—

7.

THE PLANET BLOWS UP

2.

ON A ROCK, ONE SURVIVOR...

1.

An angel or
a hand
with wings arrives

0.

FLIK—
Sends the man
into space—YAA!!!

no footing, formless

-1.

Angel smiles—
a ventriloquist's
hand painted with lips

LATER...THE ARTIST—

5. City-as-School

Day-trips
in Washington Sq
Park, dropping

out—STONED
ON SAMO. Two hits
of acid a day

& each night
his father Gerard
worrying. Searches

the weeks high
& low. Finds his son
deep in a dice

game with God.
Blood
shot. Drags Basquiat

like a cigarette
back to Bklyn
to his high school

in the city—
"Papa I'll be very very
famous one day"

delirious Basquiat
declares. Hard
headed, mama's boy,

spleenless—
on a double
dare from Al Diaz,

fills a box with Papa's
shaving cream,
at graduation giving

Principal a white face
full of menthol.
NO POINT

IN GOING BACK—smart
ass Basquiat empties
his locker, heads

for the big city
with Papa's cash
loan. GOOD PLACE

FOR A HANDOUT.
EASY MARK
SUCKER. SURVIVING

CHILD WITH SEED OF LIFE—
knows only how to move
forward like a shark

or an 8-track, going
out of style. For broke.
PLUSH SAFE HE THINK:

Only the good
die numb—Bird
& Billie & Jimi

& Jesus—
his heroes
crowned

like a tooth.
GOLD WOOD.
Basquiat begins

with hisself, writes
FAMOUS
NEGRO ATHLETES

on downtown walls,
spraying SAMO
across SoHo—

"royalty, heroism
& the streets"—
covering galleries

with AARON
& OLD TIN. ORIGIN
OF COTTON. NO

MUNDANE OPTIONS.

6. Vocabulario

cabal
caballero
cacao

cadáver
café
cambio

¡caramba!
carbón
caribe

Carmen
carnaval
carnívoro

catecismo
célebre
celibato

censor
centrífugo
cerveza

César
cicatriz
ciudad

civilización
combustible
complexión

cómplice
conductibilidad
corazón

corrosivo
cuba
chimpancé

chocolatería

7. Brothers Sausage   { 1983 }

The trees told nobody
what, that day, we did—
we died. Laid down

with our cans
of deviled
ham & closed

our eyes—two
valises full
of Van Camp's

Pork & Beans—
the city an idea
shining far behind—

& we were not afraid

just terrified
of bears, of basic
black—the night—

white hunters
with their plaid
& pop-guns—

sleep was our bag—
a body—we began
to crave our beds

even empty & unmade
as a mind—
the silence & sounds

of nature scared us—

WORLD WORLD
FAMOUS—
EST 1897

COTTON,
SLAVES, IN MAY A
DERANGED—

this Indian
land given
no heed, taken

back & turned to park—

BEEF PORK SALT
WATER CORN
SYRUP SOLIDS

guns loaded
like a question,
aimed—imagine—

shhhh—be vewy
vewy quiet, we're
hunting wabbits—

DARWIN.
ALLAH. BUDDHA.
BLUE RIBBON.

MALCOLM X
VS. AL JOLSON—
whistling Dixie,

we pack up
like meat—ACME—
to the city—

8. Man-Made

WELL
  KEPT
    WHITE

CADILLAC—
  Basquiat dead
    broke on Saint

Mark's, marketing
  his postcards
    like coke

AN ADVERTISEMENT
  FOR SODA
    crashing out

at friend's pads,
  wherever he can.
    THIS GRAPH SHOWS

A TRIPLING OF FIVE
  TO SIX MILLION
    NEW

AND EXISTING UNITS
  WITHOUT PLUMBING.
    Crammed with pals

in photo booths
  taking shots
    WE HAVE DETERMINED

THE BULLET WAS GOING
  VERY FAST—collages
    the Warren Commision,

THE TEAM: RUNS
  HITS
    ERRORS.

Tries to hock
  his J. Edgar Hoover,
    Jack Ruby shooting

or a postcard flag
  to Henry Gedzahler
    & Andy Warhol

lunching
　　at WPA—
　　　　Too young

is all the cultural
　　commissioner offers—
　　　　IT TOOK THE GUILT

OF 4 GENERATION OF SWEATSHOP WORKER
　　TO GAIN ACCESS
　　　　TO THE STATESMAN—

but Warhol buys some dance.
　　MILLIONAIRE$.
　　　　15 PER CENT—

Here's a tip—
　　sleep
　　　　where you can

till they can't
　　stand
　　　　you no more—

cover the doors
　　the fridge
　　　　BEFORE THE CRANES

LIFT THEM
　　OF THE EDGE
　　　　OF THE 3-STORY

UNIT
　　till slumlord
　　　　tosses you out. LOVE.

A GIANT GORILLA
　　LYING
　　　　ON THE PAVEMENT.

His name not yet
　　nailed up,
　　　　neoned, across town

or bannered
　　on the backs
　　　　of bi-planes—

he hustles sweat-
   shirts hand
      painted—abstract

on front
   MAN-MADE©
      in back.

Cooks up schemes
   like stash.
      Technician

mad scientist
   scorcerer's apprentice—
      SAMO© must be

a white cat, they say,
   some conceptual artiste—
      couldn't be B,

this black kid in a lab
   coat & blond
      mohawk

with afro in the back—
   SAMO© AS AN END
      2 BOOSH-WAH-

ZEE FANTASIES—
   his arrow-head
      or weathervane

pointing out—away—

There had been a lot of talk that the graffiti writer named SAMO was a white conceptual artist—everybody was up on conceptual stuff in the '70s. And then this black guy comes in and everybody's like "Yo Fred, SAMO's here." And the guy who was organizing this whole scam, which he was calling Canal Zone, tried to pit us against each other. I remember Jean had this big smile on his face. He had a blond mohawk that came to a point at the tip of his forehead, and the rest of his head was shaved in the front, and the back portion was still intact. It was very bizarre. He had on a white smock, which was dingy and paint-splattered, and raggedy shoes, and he came in smiling. Lee and I looked at him and smiled, and it was like…there's a thing in the graffiti world, which is that people know who you are before they meet you. The writers are always happy to meet other writers. Jean-Michel was a writer, and he was a fan of ours, and we were fans of his.

—FAB 5 FREDDY
(Fred Braithwaite)

10. Gringo Pilot   { 1981 }

SAMO© ESTA
EN ALGO—
equals he's up

to something,
mentioned with Al
in the *Voice*,

first name only.
BOOSH-WAH-
ZEE OR CIA?

His atomic
hairdo, short
in front, dreads

out back, sorties
over the city—
ANOLA GAY

ANOLA GAY
BBBB
He's on

something—dive bombs

& bars. SAMO©
AS SOLUTION
TO PLAYING ART

WITH DADDY'S MONEY.
B not yet launched,
counting down, out—

Declaration Value

¿DISEASE CULTURE?

Customs—
Will his eagle
ever fly? number

ever hit—come in—
Yanqui, Americon,
Tuskegee Airman—

or will he lift
off, then—mayday—
drop, burnt

by backlash
his body black
chalk on

a sidewalk? Hop
scotch, skelly
court, scene of murder

rehearsed—TAR
tar aspuria.
Trinity

Test, Fat Man,

Little Boy—unstable
isotope,
fissionable core—

Rita Hayworth taped
to the bombshell. Exit
Row. Do not write

on the back. Write
English with all capital
letters. Keep form

until departure from
U.S.—
deported, interred,
interrogated, dis-

missed, he's on

to something—
Gringo, Nuyorican,
loco

loco—
has a fall
out with Al Diaz.

1. Apellido
2. Nombre
3. Fecha de nacimiento
   (dia/mes/año)

PUERTO RICO PEURTO
8. U.S. Address
DISNEYLAND HOTEL—

When Keith Haring
the Unknown
lets the black kid

in, past the gate
at School Visual
Art—*Las pipas*

y los cigarros
nunca se permitten—
is surprised

hours later to find
wet paint like a plane's black
box—

SAMO© IS DEAD—

his mark made
RESPO MUNDIAL—
ASBESTOS—on the wall.

11. 3 Kinds of Fences

He's begun
clearing
walls, fences

1. Barbed
   wire—
   like a baseball

   slugger—sky—
   score—
   A NEGRO PORTER

   IN A POST-DEPRESSION
   MOVIE—
   a talkie, a picture

   show measured
   in millimeters
   like a machine

   gun—IN HUSH
   HUSH TERMS
   A BLACK

   MARKET VALISE.
2. Picket—
   a line

   drive to the Green
   Monster—
   out in left

   field. Foul.
   1 WIN
       1 LOSS.

   Take him out
   of the ball
   game Take him

   out the park—
   A FRAME
   OF BUTTERED

POPCORN—
sandlots, stick
ball, cracker

jacked & all—
Free Inside
a prize,

piñatas
of possibility
3. Chain

link—
swung at
blind—

12. Monarchs

Kansas City's Own
World Colored Champions

1920

Arumi	rf, 2b	
Blukoi, Frank	2b	Philippines
Carr, George ("Tank")	1b, rf	California
Curry, Reuben "Rube"	p	Kansas City
Drake, Bill "Plunk"	p, rf	Sedalia, Mo.
Hawkins, Lemuel "Hawk," "Hawkshaw"	1b	Georgia
Jackson		
Johnson, Oscar "Heavy"	c	Atchison, Kans.
Johnson, Roy "Bubbles"	2b	Detroit
Lightner	p	
McNair, Hurley "Bugger"	p, lf	
Mathol, Carroll "Dink"	2b	
Mendez, José "Mendy"	p, 2b, mgr	Cuba
Moore, Walter "Dobie"	ss	
Ray, Otto "Jaybird"	rf, c	
Rodriguez, J	c	Cuba
Rogan, Wilbur "Bullet Joe"	p, rf	Oklahoma City
Washington, "Blue"	1b	

1922

Allen, Newton "Colt"	2b	Austin, Texas
Anderson, Theodore "Bubbles"	2b	
Joseph, Walter "Newt"	inf	Muskogee, Okla.
Sweatt, Geo. "The Teacher"	1b, 2b	Humboldt, Kans.
Taylor, Big	p	
Williams, Henry	c	Oklahoma
Yokum	p	Ash Grove, Mo.

1925

Allen, Newt	2b	

Rogan, Bullet Joe	p	
Williams, Henry	c	
Young, Tom "T.J."	c	Wichita, Kans.

1927

Allen, Newt	ss	
Everett	ss	
Orange, Grady	utility	
Young, Maurice "Doolittle"	p	
Young, Tom	c	
Young, William (Tom's brother)	p	Wichita

1929

Allen, Newt	2b	
Rogan, Bullet Joe	cf, p, mgr	
Young, Tom	c	

1931

Allen, Newt	2b	
Byas, Richard "Subby"	c, cf	
Harris, Chick "Moocha"	p, lf	
Stearnes, Norman "Turkey"	of	Detroit
Thompson, Samuel "Sad Sam"	p	
Young, Tom	c	

1932

| Bell, James "Cool Papa" | of | |

1935

Allen, Newt	2b, capt	
Brown, Willard "Big Bomb"	ss, 3b	Shreveport, La.
Kransen (Kranson, Cranston) Floyd	p	
Rogan, Bullet Joe	utility	
Trouppe, Quincy	cf	Georgia
Young, Tom	c	

1936

Allen, Newt	2b	
Else, Harry "Speedy"	c, p	
Harris, Curtis "Popsickle" "Popeye"	1b, utility	
Paige, Leroy "Satchel"	p	Mobile
Webster	p	
Wilson, Woodrow "Bo" "Lefty"	p	

1937

Allen, Newt	2b	
Johnson, Byron "Jewbaby"	ss	
Mays (referred to as Ed, Tom, Dave)		

1938

Adams, "Packinghouse"	3b	
Allen, Newt	2b	
Bowe, Randolph "Bob" "Lefty"	p	
Jackson, "Big Train"	p	
Moses	p	Farmerville, La.
O'Neil, John "Buck"	1b, rf	Sarasota, Fla.
Strong, Ted	ss	Chicago

1940

Allen, Newt	2b	
Barnes, V.	of	Hub, Miss.
Matchett, Jack "Zip"	p	Odessa, Tex.

1941

Allen, Newt	ss, 3b, mgr	
Johnson, "Cliff" "Connie"	p	Stone Mountain, Ga.
Stong, Ted	3b, rf	
Young, Tom	c	

1943

Allen, Newt	utility	
Barnhill, David "Impo"	p	
Souell, Herbert "Baldy"	3b	

1944

Allen, Newt	1b, 1f	
Bumpus, Earl	rf	Kentucky
Rivers	cf	
Young, Edward "Ned" "Pep"	c	

1945

Gray	c	
Moody, Lee	1b, cf	
Paige, Satchel	p	
Renfroe, Othello "Chico"	lf, 2b	
Robinson, John "Jackie" (traded Brooklyn Dodgers)	ss	Cairo, Ga.
Young, Leandy	of	Shreveport, La.

Before Baird sold the franchise 1955, he sold
8 Monarchs to the majors & 4 to the minors.
The details of transactions not reported.

OLEOMARGARINE   The White Bread's Burden.
From Eng. *olio,* a mixture, and Grk. *margino,* to be furious.
A furious mixture.

—*The Foolish Dictionary*
1904

13. Oleo

Between Follies
the funniest
man alive

or dead, emerges—
his behind
feathered, legs

a rooster's—
Mama's Little Baby
Loves Shortenin

Shortenin
Mama's Lil Baby Loves
Shortnin Bread—

come a mighty long
way from Walker
& Williams'

Authentic Coon
Revue—Walker
the dancing dandy

& Wms in cork
for *Sons of Ham.*
OLEO. LARD. Hamming

it up. Now
for Ziegfield
Mr Williams eats

alone, not allowed
front doors
or full billing—

may bring the house
down, but must
come in the back—

a separate room,
nothing
personal, mind

you, just house
rules—where he puts on
his face—

TRICK BLACK SOAP.
In his own light
skin, he's no one's

idea of funny
—plain brown wrapper—
but blacked up

Uncle Eggs delivers—
does his olio
between the show

girls, all ostrich
& boas, gloves
mortician white,

sight
gags before curtains
these scalped seats.

14. Gray

This now in—

On White St
those BAD
FOOLS! once known

as Test
Pattern, then
Channel 9

gig the Mudd
Club. Net-
work it—

PROSPEROUS SON
OF A BUSINESS MAN
PLAYING CLARINET—

Basquiat sticks
to the reeds, some mean
synth. Feed

back. Drum. Rock,
scissors, rolling
papers—here B

a star, his band
radio—ham—
ambulance-music.

WHY DO TV INTERVIEWER
IN PRTC TAKE
THE OPINON OF THE MOST

POSSIBLE IGNORANT PERSN—

Bottles being thrown
little dancing—the boos
begin—

but the show
ain't over till Fat
Albert sings—*hey*

heh hay. Our top story—

Now called
Gray the band's
DJ plays, scratches

the surface—
B fiddles a guitar
with a file. Amped up,

this tin can band
goes to town—GET UP
AND TALK OURSELVES

ON A BIG STAGE.
*Nah nah
nah, we're gonna*

have a good time—

THERE'S A SONG ON THE RADIO
WHERE THEY SAY WAVY HAIR
INSTEAD OF BLACK

CONSIDERABLE CLOUDINESS
~~SO~~ IT WAS SUNG BY SOME WHITEGIRLS
20 YEARS LATER.

Mushmouf
on the mike, singing
lead. STATIC IS HARD

ON VOICES BUT BLOCKS
OUT CHAOS
ON THE RUNWAY—

This is just a test.

One day he will
get a good gig
on Crosby St

or someone's basement
KERNELS OF CORN AS A FINAL OFFER
~~FOR DEFECTIVE RIFLES~~

& quit. Tonight
on a dead end
street, in the shadow of the World

Trade Ctr
CRUCIFIX TRANSMITTING
INTO 20,000 TELEVISIONS

he is the hot young
thing, newsmaker
& taker—It's 10 o'

clock America, do you know
—We interrupt this pro-
gram—who your children are?

15. New York/New Wave

RINSO

Grace—that's Miss
Jones to you—
done up

like the devil, old
Kali. Collared,
leopard

skinned—crouched
in a cage
her white photographer

& husband, placed
her in. Big
game. THE MOST

AMAZING DEVELOPMENT
IN SOAP
HISTORY. Butcher,

Maker, Josephine Baker
walked her leopards,
leashed, down

the Champs-Elysées
head high. KINGFISH.
SAPPHIRE. *I'm not*

perfect
but I'm perfect
for you—keeping

up, Jones goes
wild like a card.
Spade. THEM

SHOVELS. Joker,
queen, deuce
deuce—face

painted blue
by Warhol, her body
done in

white by Haring—
same as Bill T
Jones (no reln)

his cock striped
white, skunked.
Vein.

What a doll—
she wants to wear
Haring's radiant

babies, pale crosses,
tribal headdress
& all, to the ball. Little

else. Cinder-
ella has nothing
on Grace—

NO SUH
NO SUH
princess

& step-
sister rolled
into one. IL FOOL.

SLOGAN.
If the soft
shoe fits...

Diva, devil
may care—
she's riding high

as fashion. *Love*
is the drug
& she's here

to score.
~~SAPPHIRE©.~~
Slave

to the rhythm, rinse
—repeat—WHITE
WSHING ACTION—

THE WOLVES

Hey there
girl—buffalo gal—
painted gold

on the album
BOW WOW
WOW—

head shaved
poodled
on the sides

Go wild
Go wild! Go
wild in the country!

Naked—no,
nude
like Goldfinger

girl (who they
say died in real
life, suffocated

by her skin
painted gold)
midasized—

Odd Job
with his bowler
that boomeranged

razor-sharp back
—HALF NELSON—
ruff. What color's

that skin
you're in, gold
peeled like bark

bite? YUP
GRRRR
WELL YOU NEED'NT

How'd they pick
you, cottoned, out
the crowd & where

you at now?
The place we
all end—99¢

bin, potter's
field—SALE—full
of bones even tame

dogs bury like bank
robber's loot.
I want candy—

her skin a lottery
scratch n'
sniff—win—

or sorry—try again—

16. New York Beat   { 1980–81 }

Glenn O'Brien, dir.
Maripol, prod.

Gone from TV
Party to Great Jones
from special guest

to star, he's hooked
up — his first
crash pad—

the film's production
office. Catches sleep
like fire—PAY

FOR SOUP—
wakes to paint, playing
a day in the life

of artist
to the hilt. TILT—
his name up in

lights, smoke, the script
improvised, pin-
balled along. Body

English. MATCH.
Racks up
canvas & art

supplies—BUILD
A FORT—
trying to score

the ladies—
no dice. Add coins
to play. FIRST

AMBITION FIREMAN

FIRST ARTISTIC
CARTOONIST.
Among Blondie & electric

boogaloo, lies
his big break—head
spinning—scratch—able

to buy paint, a bit
of pot—he's stoked
SET THAT

ON FIRE—& some start
to notice. Blondie
buys her a small canvas

& he's dancing
with zoot-
suited, mustachioed

Kid Creole, making eyes
at the beached
Coconuts—brown out

& white inside—
cool as milk.
APOSTLE, ROT,

LIKE AN IGNORANT
EASTER SUIT.
He's busting up

& out, till the Italian
backers go bankrupt—
THE WHOLE LIVERY

LINE BOW LIKE
THIS—losing his roof
his flophouse fee, left

B holden
the bag. All that's kept
are some stills

& Maripol's Polaroids
of him shimmer
-ing—the film

SELF-PAINTINGS 6AM
like life
left unfinished.

17. Times Square Show

group show, 41st and Seventh Ave.
June 1980

He's lit
    thru the Apple—
that sweet scent

    of tar—

    •

    Gone for 5 min.

    •

EVEN BOHEMIANS
EVEN BOHEMIANS
EVEN BOHEMIANS LOVE RAZU

    •

    We may doze
    —but—
    never close

    •

SAMO© AS AN END
2 NINE
2 FIVE CLONES

    •

Outside the show, like a dog
he hangs
a sign FREE SEX

till too much biz
drops through
& it has to come down

    •

    Clowns for Hire

    •

    Girls Girl Girl

•

Soap-smeared
windows
To Let

•

A PENAL CAMP
WITH CIGARETTES, GIRLS
AND DANCING——

•

Dogwalker Available
Polish-American Girl.
Lots of experience

with all
sorts of dogs
References Avail.

•

Metal gates gape—
braces in rich girl's
mouth or bar brawler

with his jar wired shut
—either way
silent

•

Bill of Rights:

No smoking or incense
A courteous, English-speaking driver
A radio-free (silent) trip

•

DICTATOR
TATOR
AMOR

•

Lady Pink
struts her Holzer
shirt—

Abuse
of Power
Comes as No Surprise

—the lights behind her blurred

•

PROCTOR & GAMBLE

•

fresh piss & dogshit

•

We pay highest

•

Sold $25—
Amersterdam Ave
Greater Jones

—& a handshake

•

LEAD DUST
FOR THREE $
AN / HOUR

•

Keys
Locks
We make dupes

•

FLOUR
CUT FLOUR WITH IT
FLOUR

•

Heros Hot
& Cold

109. Breakdancing. The streets of the ghetto have been one of the recent word-factories of English, on both sides of the Atlantic.

—*The Story of English*

18. Beyond Words

Mudd Club 4th floor gallery
Manhattan, April 1981

If you bomb
the IND
or tag the 2

downtown
—gallery-bound—
dousing it in tribal

shrapnel, you're it
—the shit—
If you can lie

between the rails
—Please Stand
Clear the Closing—

or press yourselves
betw. train
& the wall

spray can rattling
like a tooth—*The roof*
the roof

the roof is on
fire—soon
the 6 will whistle

past, swinging
like a night stick—
Officer Pup throwing

a brick
@ that Mouse
Ignatz, in love—

#$!?!!!!—then
you'll have found
risk. A calling—

Crash, Daze, Pray
covering trains
like cave paintings,

avoiding the German
shepherds—ACHTUNG—
while the cars sit

in the yards
—what no one else in this
city owns. Making

their names
known—Dondi, Boy-
5, B-Sirius, Crazy

Legs, Coolie C—
The city clears
its throat

the subway shaking
the buildings above—
We don't need

no water let
the motherfucker
burn—Futura 2000,

Phase II, Quick
& Sex & Zephyr
& Lady Pink—

Fab 5 Freddy
(né Braithwaite)
saying everyone's

a star. "Rapture" —

the whole planet's in
on it— Chilly Most
Being the Host Coast

to Coast—Freddy's painted
Campbell's Soup Cans that read
DADA & POP instead

of beef barley—
the UFO has landed
& a brother's

stepped out, alien, dressed
in white. *Then when*
there's no more cars

he goes out at night
& eats up bars—
graffiti like 3 card monte—

running, avoiding the pigs
like a black muslim
bean pie. *DJ spinning*

says my my.
Pay attn.—
say, ain't that

Basquiat spinning

disks behind Blondie—
SAMO© AS AN END
TO MINDWASH RELIGION—

45s stacked high
as a Dag-
wood sammich?

Hungry, this B-
boy's headed
to the top—*Yes*

Yes y'all
You don't stop—
blowing up.

Jean-Michel is proud of his large *Samo* Tag in a schoolyard, surrounded by other Tags on top of Tags, yet not marked over. This demonstrates respect for the artist as not just a graffitist but as an individual, the worth of whose Tag is recognized. There's prestige in not being bombed over. There are also fake *Samo*s and Harings as well as a counter-Haring graffitist who goes around erasing him.

—RENE RICARD
"The Radiant Child"

19. Defacement { 1983 }

acrylic & ink on wallboard
25 x 30 in.

Basquiat scrawls
& scribbles, clots
paint across

the back
wall of Keith Haring's
Cable Building studio—

two cops, keystoned,
pounding a beat,
pummel

a black face—scape
goat, sarcophagus—
uniform-blue

with sticks. The night
Michael Stewart snuck
on the tracks

& cops caught him
tagging
a train—THIRD RAIL

DANGER LIVE
VOLTAGE—
taught him better

than to deface public
property. Choke
hold. Keep NEW YOKE

CITY Clean.
Give those men
a PABST BLUE

RIBBON, a slap
on the wrist
a meddle

of honor. Basquiat
produces *Beat
Bop,* black

on black
vinyl—VOCAL.
TEST PRESSING.

INTESTINES.
TARTOWN
RECORDS. EAR.

All revolutions
33 1/3.
When Haring moves

up & out, he'll tear
down that wall
careful to get

Basquiat out intact—
in Haring's
bedroom modeled

after the Ritz
¿DEFACEMENT?
sits, saved

like a face, framed—

20. Six Crimee

1.

The drugs were, we are
told, smuggled swallowed
by the couple discovered

—no canine could—
only by X-ray
& laxative

2.

Height Weight
Age Hair Race
Approximate

3.

When he regained

conscience, came to—

found his ID's missing

4.

After the alleged
kidnapping
police conducted

a sweep rounded up

some teenagers
a math teacher
a father of two

none fit
the suspect
's descript

Mayor swore
swift justice
for the perp

etrator Police Chief
wanted to get
the bottom, sought

a thorough invest-
igation Officers
involved promoted

with pay all charges
later dropped
or never brought bought

5.

The one thief
to the right
pocketed the nail

to his palm

sparing God
pain
—Thus, gypsies

(see under Bohemia)

allowed
to tell fortunes
& lies

6.

Your life this
way moves
& that—small

time dealer
getaway
car driver—

sirens on

your tail—sacks
full of well
marked bills

& a flat
tire on the road
out of town—stuttering

engine—on foot
iambic—sprung—
you are found out

finished. Put
your hands where
we can see them

assume position—

trussed up
like a trout, gotten
clean—hands

finger-printed—
nails stained
herring-red

21. Irony of Negro Policeman   { 1981 }

His inked arm—
proud, pea-
cocked, preening

like a teenager—
PLCMN
placed above

PAW (LEFT),
a pawn.
Drawn

& quartered—
arm half-mast
a flag

—not a fist—
2-WAY
WRIST

RADIO—
cuffed,
resists—

22. Obnoxious Liberals { 1982 }

From left to right—

ASBESTOS ASBESTOS
    ASBESTOS
       around the cut head

of Samson—Abraham
    Lincoln with his hands
       raised, tophat on,

arrow-armed—
    NOT FOR SALE
       across his chest

like Superman's S—
    last, a plantation
       owner in Hawaiian

shorts, broad-
    brimmed hat,
       a tan grin—

shoulders double
    dollar signs—
       $ $

like an epaulet—

23. Dos Cabezas   { 1982 }

*former collection
of Andy Warhol*

Cabezas means friends
or so we thought—the gap
in Basquiat's teeth

What me worry?
a generation
between both men—

Warhol with hand raised
pensing or perhaps
picking his nose—

Basquiat's snout flat
broad brushstrokes, hair
bushy. Right after

meeting official Warhol,
B headed
back home to paint

the pair, returning
to Andy's Factory,
the canvas still wet

as a kiss. A gift. Sold
at auction their faces fetch
five times the asking—

feeding frenzy
over the newly
& nearly

dead—*Do I hear
a hundred thousand*—
not two friends

we learned
but two—translated—
heads.

Fighters, you may say, are born, whilst champions are made—in Fleet Street and the complementary thoroughfares of New York and San Francisco. A particular boxer is discussed in some newspaper every day for a considerable period. He is advertised, in fact. You get accustomed to the fellow's name in exactly the same way as you get accustomed to the name of some coffee or toffee, tailor or tinker. You begin to regard him, quite unconsciously, as an inevitable concomitant of everyday life. And when the paper tells you that he is a champion, you, having a general interest in boxing but knowing very little about it, accept him as a champion.

—BOHUN LYNCH
Knuckles & Gloves
1923

24. Amateur Bout

PSALM

Blood in his mouth
this morning, high
cotton, a prize

fight—trying
to beat this thing,
breathe easy

as money.
THIS IS NOT
IN PRAISE

OF POISON
ING MYSELF
WAITING FOR IDEAS

TO HAPPEN—MYSELF —
THIS   NOT
          IS

IN PRAISE OF POISON
THIS   IS NOT
                    NON

·

He's full
as his notebook
—with worry

His mouth
shoots
off like craps

"ANDY'S TRAP
NO DICE
STRICTLY CASH

PAIGET WATCHES"
this sick counter
clockwork, up

& downers—

·

57

TRUE STORY

SHOT A FOOL'S
"SHOT A FOOL'S
HEAD OFF"!

~~JAIL LINGO~~
Now this shot
to his arm

's got him
possumed, doing
the rope-a-dope

•

A PRAYER

NICOTINE WALKS
ON EGGSHELLS
MEDICATED

THE EARTH WAS
FOR   LESS
FORMLESS VOID—

his furnaced
breath, his iron
lung

DARKNESS FACE
OF THE DEEP
SPIRIT MOVED ACROSS

THE WATER
AND THERE
WAS LIGHT

"IT WAS GOOD"©

BREATHING INTO HIS
LUNGS 2000 YEARS
OF ASBESTOS

WAX SEAL
LINE
STAMP

VERY OFFICIAL
"FOR THE SICKLES
FOR THE MATTOCKS

FOR THE FORKS
FOR THE AXES"
SHINING SHOE

IN ST LOUIS
THE NON POISONOUS
POISONED

SO SELF RIGHTOUS
NO ONE IS CLEAN
FROM RED MEAT TO WHITE

Sex smell
of the smoke-
house

Sauce stains
like paint
on pale aprons

THIS NOT IN PRAISE
OF ~~POISON~~
THE BIGGEST BUISNESS

UGLY, FAT LIKE A PIG

•

LOVE IS A LIE

LOVER = LIAR

•

NEON SHOE REPAIR

He alphabets
east—Ave A,
C, D—

LOTTERY
CANDY
MAGAZINES

CIGARS©
Got a late
night jones

Sleepwalks
awake, high-
strung

along the ropes—
come out swinging
"ARAB SINGING"

& prayer from above
EFFECTIVE 12:01 AM
Make the rounds

trying to score
a TKO, the gate
big as a welter

weight's—A MICKEY
FINN WITH
FUZZ ON IT IN

A TURKISH BATH
In this corner
of Loisaida

ROACH EGGS
  ROACH EGGS
    ROACH EGGS

ROACH EGGS

he wants to strike
some blows

score that heavy belt

•

PEEL

NOT IN PRAISE
NOT IN PRAISE
OF POISON

He's off
like a bet—dime
bag, training

bag, punch
drunk & judy—
a hit—

THE CUSTOMER
IN NEW YORK,
CHICAGO, DETROIT

•

JUNK AND CIGARETTES

25. Oxidation Portrait
of Jean-Michel Basquiat { 1982 }

How many people
          did Warhol pay
                    or over lunch ask

to piss across
          the canvas,
                    its silk-

screen of Basquiat,
          hair in Mickey
                    Mouse knots?

How long
          till the urine
                    fought

the copper
          paint, began
                    to rust?

rot? before
          his portrait
                    grew green

& gold, spotting
          his face
                    like liver,

a leopard, like years
          later, spleen
                    gone, the heroin

started to eat,
          stark communion,
                    his skin?

26. Dimensions

Jean-Michel Basquiat
(American, 1960-1988),
Untitled (1960),

1982. Acrylic
oil paintstick & paper
collage on wood, 36

x 24 in. Courtesy
Robert Miller Gallery,
New York. ©

Estate of Jean-Michel
Basquiat. Printed
in Germany. Used

by permission. All
right reserved.

27. VNDRZ   { 1982 }

Antennae, antlers,
rabbit ears
for better reception—

Basquiat's hair
a bundle of dread-
locks, coiled, clenched

in two fists
above his head.
A matador's hat.

No pick, no make
up, just a shark
skin suit on a throne

that's held half
of Harlem—a Siamese
on his lap,

looking sidelong.
MOST YOUNG KINGS
GET THEIR HEADS

CUT OFF. No coon-
skin coats
or homemade back

drops, JMB
sharp & wrinkled
like VanDerZee's

ninetysomething
hands, head tucked
beneath a black

hood, the light,
shrouded—days
later agitates

in complete
dark—Basquiat
bobbing up

from chemicals
to the surface,
face forming

64

like a ghost—exposed,
fixed, washed. Right
before the year buries

our photographer,
Basquiat paints
VNDRZ—his bouquet

of hands, a staff
of a man, rod
full of lightning

striking that
knotted, volted,
vaulted name.

Side **2** Hits

DISC **1**: ZYDECO

28. NEGATIVE.
29. JACK JOHNSON.
30. NOTARY PUBLIC.
31. THE FUN GALLERY.
32. 2 1/2 HOURS OF CHINESE FOOD.
33. PORK.
34. EYES & EGGS. 1983.
35. TELEVISION & CRUELTY TO ANIMALS.
36. QUALITY MEATS FOR THE PUBLIC.
37. OUT GETTING RIBS.
38. SHADOW BOXING: *works on canvas*
39. B.O.
40. IN ITALIAN: *a trip*
41. ONION GUM. 1983.

42. WINE OF BABYLON. 1984.
43. BATTLE ROYALE: *may the best man win*
44. FIRST CLASS. 1983.

{ Quality Meats for the Public }

As much as undervaluation can kill, so can a false sense of the value of your work. Jean-Michel was advised to stop giving it away. But if your friends can't have it, why live?

—RENE RICARD

28. Negative

Wake to find everything black
what was white, all the vice
versa—white maids on TV, black

sitcoms that star white dwarfs
cute as pearl buttons. Black Presidents,
Black Houses. White horse

candidates. All bleach burns
clothes black. Drive roads
white as you are, white songs

on the radio stolen by black bands
like secret pancake recipes, white back-up
singers, ball-players & boxers all

white as tar. Feathers on chickens
dark as everything, boiling in the pot
that called the kettle honky. Even

whites of the eye turn dark, pupils
clear & changing as a cat's.
Is this what we've wanted

& waited for? to see snow
covering everything black
as Christmas, dark pages written

white upon? All our eclipses bright,
dark stars shooting across pale
sky, glowing like ash in fire, shower

every skin. Only money keeps
green, still grows & burns like grass
under dark daylight.

29. Jack Johnson

1982, acrylic & oil paintstick
on canvas

Jack decided that being a painter was less of a vocation than he
had supposed. He would be a boxer instead. He had the punch;
he had the speed; he was capable of moving half a second before
trouble arrived in his neck of the woods.

—DENZIL BATCHELOR
Jack Johnson & His Times

BLACK JACK: *b. 31 March 1878*

Some call me spade,
stud, buck, black. That last
I take as compliment—

"I am black & they
won't let me forget it."
I'm Jack

to my friends, Lil'
Arthur—like that King
of England—to my mama.

Since I got crowned champ
most white folks would love
to see me whupped.

They call me dog, cad
or card, then bet
on me to win. I'm still

an ace & the whole
world knows it. Don't
mean most don't want

me done in. But I got words
for them too—when I'm through
most chumps wish

they were counting
cash instead
of sheep, stars. I deal

blows like cards—
one round, twenty
rounds, more. "I'm black all

right & I'll never let them
forget it." Stepping
to me, in or out

the ring, you gamble—
go head then dealer,
hit me again.

And there had come into prominence a huge negro, Jack
Johnson, who was anxious to fight Burns. In England we had
hitherto heard very little of Johnson. He was three years older
than the white champion, stood 6 feet and one-half inch, and
weighed 15 stone. He appears to have started his career in 1899,
and from that year down to December, 1908, when he finally
succeeded in getting a match with Burns, he had fought sixty-
five contests, half of which he won by means of a knock-
out. ...He was very strong, very quick, a hard hitter, and extraor-
dinarily skilful in defence. He was by no means unintelligent,
and not without good reason, was regarded generally with the
greatest possible dislike. With money in his pocket and physical
triumph over white men in his heart, he displayed all the gross
and overbearing insolence which makes what we call the buck
nigger insufferable.

—BOHUN LYNCH
Knuckles & Gloves
1923

THE UPSET: *26 December 1908*

"Who told
you I was yellow?"
I wanted to know

taunted— "Come
& get it
Lil Tahmy"

in my best English
accent, inviting
Burns to dodge

my fists the way
he'd avoided me,
running

farther —Britain
France—than
that kangaroo

I once bet I could
outdistance & did.
Chased down

to Sydney
Stadium, now was nowhere
to go—no more

color line to hide
behind, no lies bout
my coward streak—

I will bet a few plunks
the colored man
will not make good!

That I wasn't game.
Baited him
like a race—first

round he fell
with his odds,
favored. By two

all bets were even
& I made him pay—drew
blood—pounded

his face into morse, worse
than what Old Teddy
Roosevelt could stand

to hear over the wire. Bully.
"You're white, dead
scared white

as the flag of surrender.
You like to eat
leather?" By twelve I bet

he wished
he was still
at sea, had stayed Noah

Brusso, not Burns
trapped in Rushcutters Bay
about to be smoked

like my finest
cigar. "Didn't
they tell us this

boy was an in-
fighter?"
By thirteen

rounds he bites
luck & dust—
the police

rush in like fools,
angels, afraid
for both of us

treading this ring
like water,
my wide wake.

There is no use minimizing Johnson's victory in order to soothe
Burn's feelings. It is part of the game to take punishment in the
ring, and it is just as much part of the game to take unbiased crit-
icism afterwards in the columns of the Press. Personally I was
with Burns all the way. He is a white man, and so am I. Naturally
I wanted to see the white man win.

—*Jack London Reports*

THE CROWN: *4 July 1910*

In order to take
away my title
Jeffries—Great White

Hope—emerged
like a whale, lost
weight, spouted

steam. Said Negroes
have a soft spot
in our bellies

that only needs
finding. Bull's
eye. He refused

our pre-fight shake—
my eyes clear
like the time, years

later, I saw Rasputin
at the Czar's Palace
weeks before the Reds

stormed in, & knew that big
man—whom no one could
outdrink or talk—was grand

but finished. Heard
it took five tries
—poison, stabbing, more—

before he went at last
under. Jeffries was cash
by round one. Fresh

from his alfalfa
farm retirement,
only he was fool

or good enough
to challenge me, stage
a bit of revolution—

the Whites
couldn't have
me running

their show, much less
own the crown.
Called for my head.

"Devoutly hope
I didn't happen
to hurt you, Jeff"—

my fists harpoons,
hammers of John
Henry gainst

that gray engine
—*I think I can*—
steaming. Stood

whenever in my corner
facing the sun
after giving him

the shady one.
My trunks navy
blue as Reno

sky, Old Glory
lashed through
the loops—that
Independence

Day, despite warning
shots & death threats
before the match,

I lit Jeffries like black
powder, a fire
cracker—

on a breakfast
of 4 lamb cutlets
3 eggs, some steak

beat him till he
hugged me
those last rounds

& I put him
out his misery.
You could hear the riots

already—from Fort
Worth & Norfolk,
Roanoke to New

York, mobs
gather, turning
Main Street into a main

event, pummeling
any black cat
who crosses

their paths.
Neck tie
parties—cutting

another grin
below any raised
Negro chins—

JOHNSON WINS
WHITES LYNCH
70 ARRESTED

BALTIMORE
OMAHA NEGRO
KILLED—

all because I kept
their hope
on the ropes. His face

like newsprint
bruised. On account
of my coal-fed heart—

caboose red
& bright
as his—what wouldn't give.

Amaze an' Grace, how sweet it sounds,
Jack Johnson knocked Jim Jeffries down.
Jim Jeffries jumped up an' hit Jack on the chin.
An' then Jack knocked him down agin.

The Yankees hold the play,
The white man pull the trigger;
But it makes no difference what the white man say,
The world champion's still a nigger.

—TRADITIONAL

THE RING: *13 May 1913*

The bed is just
another ring I'd beat
them white boys in—

double, four
poster, queen.
I'd go the rounds

with girls who begged
to rub my head
cause it was clean

shaven, polished.
Said it felt like billiards
to them, bald

black. Balling
was fine, but once
I began to knock out

their men & sweep
the women off their feet
—even bought one a ring—

well, that was too much.
When I exchanged vows
with my second wife

—before God & everyone—
they swore I'd pay. Few
could touch me anyway,

what did I care. Later
when she did herself in
in our bed, I knew

—sure as standing—
they'd pushed her
to the edge. After

I mourned & met
my next love
& wife—my Mama,

Tiny, said
little but worry—
they trumped

up charges, 11 counts
of the Mann Act
so I couldn't fight. My dice

role came up thirteen—
a baker's dozen
of prostitution & white

slavery—a white jury
after one hour found me
guilty of crimes

versus nature. Put
me through the ringer.
Nigras, you see, ain't

supposed to have brains
or bodies, our heads just
a bag to punch. But I beat

the rap without fists—
disguised as a Black
Giant, I swapped

gloves—boxing
for baseball—traded
prison stripes for Rube

Foster's wool
uniform. Smuggled
north into Canada

like chattel, we sailed
the *Corinthian*
for England, staying below

deck. Fair France
greeted me with a force
of police—turns out to tame

the cheering crowds—
granted me amnesty,
let me keep my hide

whether world
champ, con, or stripped
like my crown.

Jack Johnson's case will be settled in due time in the courts. Until the court has spoken, I do not care to either defend or condemn him. I can only say at this time, that this is another illustration of the most irreparable injury that a wrong action on the part of a single individual may do to a whole race. It shows the folly of those who think that they alone will be held responsible for the evil that they do. Especially is this true in the case of the Negro in the United States today. No one can do so much injury to the Negro race as the Negro himself. This will seem to many persons unjust, but no one can doubt that it is true.

What makes the situation seem a little worse in this case, is the fact that it was the white man, not the black man who has given Jack Johnson the kind of prominence he has enjoyed up to now and put him, in other words, in a position where he has been able to bring humiliation upon the whole race of which he is a member.

—BOOKER T. WASHINGTON
for *United Press Association*
23 October 1912

Some pretend to object to Mr. Johnson's character. But we have yet to hear, in the case of white America, that marital troubles have disqualified prizefighters or ball players or even statesmen. It comes down then, after all, to this unforgiveable blackness. Wherefore we conclude that at present prizefighting is very, very immoral, and that we must rely on football and war for pastimes until Mr. Johnson retires or permits himself to be "knocked out."

—W.E.B. DU BOIS
Crisis, August 1914

THE FIX: *5 April 1915*

That fight with Willard was a
fix
not a faceoff. Out of the ring
three years, jonesing

for the States, I struck a deal
to beat the Mann
Act—one taste of mat

& I'd get
let back home.
But I even told

my mama—
Tiny,
Bet on me.

Once in the bout—run out
of Mexico by Pancho
Villa himself—I fought that fix

the way, years back, Ketchel
knocked me down
even after we'd shook

& agreed I'd take the fall
if he carried me
the rounds without trying

to KO—crossed,
doubled
over, I stood up & broke

his teeth like
a promise. At the root.
On the canvas

they shined, white
as a lie. But with Willard
that spring, each punch

was a sucker, every round
a gun. Loaded. Still
I fixed him—strung

him along the ropes
for twenty-five
rounds. At twenty-six

the alphabet in my head
gave way—saw
my wife take the take,

count our fifty grand
& leave. Did the dive,
shielding my eyes—

not so much from Havana
heat—its reek my favorite
cigar—as from the ref's count.

Down, I counted too, blessings
instead of bets. Stretched
there on the canvas

—a masterpiece—stripped
of my title, primed
to return to the States.

Saved. Best
believe I stood up
smiling.

If you tonight suddenly should become full-fledged Americans;
if your color faded, or the color line here in Chicago was mirac-
ulously forgotten: suppose, too, you became at the same time
rich and powerful;—what is it that you would want? What would
you immediately seek? Would you buy the most powerful of
motor cars and outrace Cook County? Would you buy the most
elaborate estate on the North Shore? Would you be a Rotarian or
a lion or a What-not of the very last degree? Would you wear the
most striking clothes, give the richest dinners and buy the
longest press notices?

—W.E.B. Du Bois
Criteria of Negro Art

Bought art
by the armful
—going out

of style
or mind—stocked
the bar full

& hired girls—
colored, white, some
you could hardly

tell—to serve
drinks & dance. Ragtime
bands, Dixieland

& a few Rembrandts
hung beside prizebelts
wide as my smile.

Hosting, hustling,
chryselephantine,
I dressed to the nines—

linen suits, white
ties, crocodile
shoes—the South

Side never saw
such finery.
Haberdashery.

Back then in
my Café de Champion
I could really put them

back—when the Levee
heard about my high
life, they demanded

prohibition, declared
us sin—wanted
to flood us out

the way Galveston, diluvian,
once tried to do me.
Still Bricktop sang nightly—

till some musician
shot me over
a white woman

whom I matrimonied
3 mos. later—
Where's your mother

Mrs Johnson? the press
pressed her. Her answer—
"I don't know

& don't care." They went
after
me with a vengeance
—lock, stock, gun

barrel—so I left
that claw-patch
of crabs, Chicago,

& went abroad, nephew
& wife
by my side. We Three

Musketeers—redoubtable—
stuck out
& stuck it out

for years—leashed
leopards—run out of more
countries than I could

count, score
of suitcases
in tow. The Great War

pushed us to Mexico
City—we drank
with generals, *científicos,*

Presidents soon deposed—
forced again north
Tijuana way

to start my Main Event
Café. Soon I tired
of opening

wine, a life of cork—
vinegared
on prizefights

& bulls & bribes—
I wanted Chi-town
back, all that

jazz. Bid
freedom farewell
at the Last Chance

Saloon, grinning, shaking
hands with arresting
officers over

the border—then faced
Stateside the same judge
who'd given me a year

& a day. *You play
square with me,
Jack & you won't find*

things too bad
said Warden
(former Governor

of Nevada, where I'd bettered
Jeffries so bad
the fight film is still banned

blockaded).
To jail
I chauffeured myself.

In the Walls
at Leavenworth
I kept cigars

& liquor & my own
private cook—fought
all-comers & Topeka

Jack Johnson—spoke
on Job, Esau, Esther,
Revelations & the virtues

of a life of moderation.
"I was always
attacking—my attack

was to counter
the leads I forced."
Homilectics

got me let out early
—caught to NYC
the 20th Century

Ltd.— engineered—
steamed—running
on good behavior.

After his high society white wife committed suicide in a cafe he owned in Chicago, Johnson married another white woman—it was no coincidence. But one could question the frame-up he faced. I mean, Jack Johnson being convicted of violating the "White Slavery Act" and being sentenced to a year and a day imprisonment...But exiled to Paris with joy—and as usual "Very Grand." It had to be Europe and they say he had a pet leopard he'd walk while drinking champagne with crowds following.

—MILES DAVIS
Jack Johnson liner notes

EXHIBITIONS

Ticker tape rain
up in Harlem—
my welcome

felt like freedom
after the tuck-tail
of jail. The day's news

tossed at my feet
the stocks
bonds. Outside

I toured my bass
viol, upright,
playing by ear—wrestling

pythons—selling
ointments & appearances.
Even spoke to a klavern

of Ku Klux
on the golden rule.
Their ovation after

sounded like Spain
& France, the crowds
who applauded

when I fought foes
who never stood
a ghost

of a chance—Arthur Craven
poet & pugilist—
or 2 horses, charging,

held by my arms
padded, wrapped in steel
locks. With Paris

showgirls I showed
off my strength, hoisted
three at a time

over my rotting
smile. But polite
as she was Europa kept me

under her opera
glass—no surprise
a zeppelin only I could see

pursued me across London
with my white
Benz & wife

once the Great War
began. Between
sparring & bull

fights & my show
Seconds Out!
I offered to spy

for the States—or the highest
bidder—but the Continent kept on
serving me orders

to leave. Eviction.
Exile. I tired. Double
agent, ex-con

artist, champ
no longer, I retired
to the States that had tried

blindsiding me like my first
fight against the Giant
at the carny—come one

come all—pay
a worn nickel, win $5
—a fortune—if you last

3 rds. Still standing
by the 2d, I was
guided by the Giant

towards the tent
& his rube waiting
with a blackjack

—I put an end
to that. Quick. Left
his eye dark. Left

town to my own
applause
the way in 'fifteen

when Moran got a good one
in—though not
his Old Mary—

I clapped with my leather mitts
—congrats—
before—left arm broken—

my right broke his nose.
Freed, I had a fancy
to play Othello

—took a fourth
wife, white
—ended up

in film *False Nobility*
rolling my eyes
like cigars. I star

now in *Aida* as an Ethiopian
King. They have me
like Selassie, decked

out in skins. In stills
I bow—awkward—
to a blackface queen.

*Do they put you
in chains?*
"If they can get them

on me, okay & good,
but I got to show up
well—can't be

a ninny." *Do you yet
know your fate?*
"They take me up

to Memphis—not
Tenn., but the old
country—a prisoner. Boy,

I mean to struggle plenty."

This contest of men with padded gloves on their hands is a sport that belongs unequivocally to the English-speaking race, and that has taken centuries for the race to develop....It is as deep as our consciousness, and is woven into the fibers of our being. It grew as our very language grew. It is an instructive passion of race. And as men to-day thrill to short Saxon words, just so do they thrill to the thud of blows of a prize fight, to the onslaught and the repulse and to the exhibition of gameness and courage. This is the ape and tiger in us, granted. But like the man in jail, it is in us, isn't it? We can't get away from it. It is the fact, the irrefragable fact. We like fighting—it's our nature. We are realities in a real world, and we must accept the reality of our nature and all its thrillableness if we are to live in accord with the real world, and those who try to get away from these realities, who by ukase will deny their existence, succeed only in living in a world of illusion and misunderstanding. These are the people who compose theatre panics, fire panics and wreck panics. They are so far out of accord with the real world that they can make no adjustment with it when the supreme moment comes.

—*Jack London Reports*

THE RACE: *d. 10 June 1945*

Always was
ahead
of myself

my time.
Despised
by whites

& blacks alike
just cause
I didn't act right.

Gave Negroes
a bad name—
shame. Was

always a swinger
a fast talker—
my rights

the kind that broke
men's jaws.
Bigot laws.

Only good
Negro is dead
broke—if only you'd

bought less
cigars, suits
—they say—spent less

time chasing
ladies, racing
cars, goggles on

as if an aviator—
back when most
white men walked, not

to mention us. Some
nervous coloreds
half-hoped

I'd lose
so's not to prove
their race

superior
then act
like it—or not—

or out—or up-
pity, whatever
that means. The man

on the street
knows who
I am—no one's

Numidian, long
lost Caucasian
as whites claimed

once I won. I am pure
Caromontee stock.
Big bucks. I spent

my life fighting—
crossing color
lines I never drew

up, dreamt. I put
the race on
check—track—no Jack,

no Joe
Louis. My arms still
too short to go

gainst God—
on this last
road, old,

I will
speed, heading
not home

but to another
show & pot
of gold—too late

to see the truck
carrying what—
swerve—

"Remember
I was a man,
& a good one"—

in hospital
interns will think me
another fancy—

only the older doctor
shall know me—dying—
my Zephyr hugging

like an opponent
in the last round
this pole

of power—utility—
my black body
thrown free—

30. Notary Public

Calling All Cars
Calling All Cars
No Money Down

Beware of Dog
All Natural
Post No Bill

Do Not Feed
the Animauls
Slippery

When Wet
Baby on Board
Thanks

Come Again
Caution
For Rent

Live Free
or Die
Chance

of Showers
Likely
Do Not Pass

Low Fat
No Fat
SAMO© SAVES

IDIOTS
Road Narrow
Trespass

& Die
Mets Break
Losing Streak

Sunken Pavement
No Shoes No Shi*t
No Dice

In Case
of Fire Do
Not Use

9 out of 10
Recommend
Must Wash Before

Returning Hands
Some Assembly
Req'd

FLATS FIX
We Install
Confidence

No Purchase
Necessary
Swim

at Own Risk
Left Lane Ends
PEDXING

Service Area
Children
at Play

Lose Weight Fast
Will Not
Be Undersold

Kids Pay
the Temperature
DO NOT DRINK

No Hazmats
STRICTLY FOR
SUGARCANE

No Auto Fishing
No Bait No Hook
C.O.D.

Colored Only
THIS NOTE
FOR ALL DEBTS

PUBLIC & PRIVATE
Reenactment
Fresh Squeezed

Satisfaction Guaranteed
FIRE WILL ATTRACT
MORE ATTENTION

THAN ANY OTHER
CRY FOR HELP
Do Not Try

This at Home
WHEN THE FOAM
BREAKS EVERY

SOFA BREAK
GLASS
TO SOUND SIRENS

Best if Used By
Your Ad Here
Names Changed

to Protect
the Innocent
Safe Sane

Humane
If You Lived Here
Burma Shave

You'd Be Home Now
Sample Free
Rinse & Repeat

Keep This & All
Drugs
Out of Reach

31. The Fun Gallery

A buzz in the air
already, Basquiat
beaming. RAY GUN

set to stun
—maximum—a hold
up in this hole

in the wall,
a billion
paintings pinned

to dry wall
like butterflies,
stomachs. He's made it

all from scratch
& paint.
The work's too low

his dealer warned—
everything should be higher
to keep up

your prices,
speed. All night
the crowds line

outside like Disneyland
& love it. Taken
over Manhattan

he's King
Kong or Mighty Joe
Young, social

climbing—gone
from trains
to scale the Empire

State. Keeping most
of the show
for hisself, hitches

a limo to Bklyn
by dawn—the armored
car hour—up

early—or late—
as if to his own
funeral—

"Papa I've made it"

hugs & hands
him a blooming
bouquet.

32. 2 1/2 Hours of Chinese Food

You have a curious smile
and a mysterious nature
The time is right to make new friends

You will be advanced socially
without any special effort
Sing & rejoice

You will be called upon to help
a friend in trouble
A friend is a present

you give yourself
You will have no problems
in your home Lucky numbers

35 37 15 6 49 27

Your cheerful outlook is one
of your assets
You never show

vulnerability You will
live long & fruitful
self assured confident

You have the ability
to adapt
to driverse situations

A liar is not believed
even though he tell
the truth

Smile when you are ready
You'll get more secure & confident
in your relationships

with co-workers
Your exotic ideas lead you
to many exciting, new adventures!

important meetings, visits
chance encounters!
Your heart pure, mind

clear, soul devout
You will have a fine
capacity for the enjoyment

of life Enthusiastic
leadership gets you
when you least expect it

You attract cultured
& artistic
people to your home

The care & sensitivity you show
towards others will return
to you Charity

begins at home
Justice next door
Don't let friends impose

work calmly & silent
Don't wait
for others to open the right

Depart not
from the path which
fate has you

assigned Pardon
is the choicest
flower of victory

God gives you
one face, you make
yourselves another

33. Pork

Ham, Sons of
Ham hock
Ham i.e. showoff

34. Eyes & Eggs   { 1983 }

Eats. Hot
cakes. Griddle
cakes. Silver

dollars. Head
cook, pepper-dark.
Dumb

waiter. Lazy
Susan. 24 SERVICE
24 SERVICE

24 —
footprints
across a canvas

apron. Rice
in the salt
like luck, over

a shoulder. Marry
the ketchup.
Today Special—

grits, links,
sweetbreads.
This is your brain.

This your brain
on drugs, scrambled
with a side

of bacon, smiling.
Mouthless.
Black JOE.

A warmer?

Order up—
Adam & Eve
on a raft, tuna

on whiskey—
WERE HAPPY
TO SERVE YOU.

Wanted Help.
We're in the weeds—
come on back

now hear?
TO INSURE
PROMPTNESS 15%.

Two bits. End
of shift, punching
out. The whites

like an eye
—eighty-sixed—
sunny, pow-

dered, poached—

A revered old teacher used to tell a true story about an experiment with chimpanzees who were set to painting. The chimps loved to paint and did so without encouragement by the hour. Then the experimenters started rewarding them with bananas. Soon our simian brothers were more interested in the reward than in the act and their painting (which was pretty good) went to hell. They sat around snorting bananas.

—WILLIAM WILSON
"The Meaning of Jean-Michel Basquiat's Life"

35. Television & Cruelty to Animals

Boy Raised by Wolves

WOFHEAD
WOLFHEAD
WOOLHEAD

White gloves—

Rocky dives
off the board
soaring hundreds

of feet
—splashdown—
into pail of water

"And now
for something
you'll really like"

Nothing up
his sleeve, not
even arms

Draws out

the hat a rabbit
Home Preg-
nancy Test

"Sorry, Charlie"

THE KENNEL
IS RUN
BY MONARCHY

On UHF
the Green Hornet
by day normal

white-guy attorney
by night fighter
of crime

Day's Vitamin Supply

His trusty
sidekicker
Kato—

chaffeur
& alibi
& butler

Batsignal in sky
MEMBER
THE ROYAL ORDER

OF MOOSE LODGE #41
Bullwinkle—
Duh—Dudley

Do Right
riding backwards
his horse—

The evil Boris
& Natasha
(Iron Curtain)

have stolen
the priceless piece
of art off

the museum wall
Which way did he go
Which way did he go

"Silly Rabbit, Trix
for Kids"
The wonderful thing

about Tiggers
Is that Tigger's
a wonderful thing—

Sugar Bear
(Black variety)
8-BALL

Hong Kong
Phooey
Number one superguy

NAPOLEONIC STEREOTYPE
AS PORTRAYED
Scatman Crothers

Faster than human eye—
Smarter than
the Avg. Bear

"Hey Boo-Boo"
Republicans—only
elephants

who forget
Casper—Friendly
Spook

Drug enforce-
ment dogs trained
on Psuedo-Human

Remains Scent
(undetectable
by humans)

The Mutual of Omaha Indian

Lassie, played
by a male
"You go girl!"

We interrupt
this telethon
Please Curb

All our animals
spade
& neuter

Each week dozens
go un-
wanted, to sleep

A mind is a terrible

How many licks
does it take, Mr Owl,
to get to the middle

The Black Panther
The Pink
Nutcracker ballet

One Banana Two
Banana Three
Banana Four

"Wonder Twin
powers"—
This complete

breakfast
FIVE CENTS
POPEYE VERSUS

LOS NAZIS

—"Activate!"
Come on down!
You're the next—

Ms Kansas hails
from state
capitol, Topeka

enjoys
poetry & horse-
back riding

If she had
one wish—
"Form of

—a pail of water!"
Josie & Pussycats
CBS eye

The Tom & Jerry Mammy

Order of Antlers
Art dealers
Heads of bull

moose hung
high
on the walls

"exposed wood supports"

Gorilla in Topeka
Famous World Zoo
whose paintings go

for high
as ten grand
a pop—

Grape Ape (x 2)

The art recovered
from the devilish duo
caper corrupt, spoiled

"Rats—foiled again"

36. Quality Meats for the Public

Grade B
has a beef
a bone to pick

teeth with.
The world inside
awaits—femur,

front lobe—body
left skinned
segmented, an orange—

Black splashed
across canvas, exposed wood
supports stretch

like an ambulance gurney—

—lift—griots left
unburied, dead
in a tree

—uneaten yams
for the birds
to embalm.

Masterpieces
slave pieces
made from old grief

& grits. Graffitti.
Come n get it—
Hominy, harm-

ony, hogs
head cheese.
Heart trouble—

Son of ham
& eggs, Son
of Sam

I am. PORK.
Packed
in ice shipped

hip
to hip. SALT.
DRY GOODS.

Trading the past
for tense, attn.,
he's uneasy as peace

—this piece
an apology, a future
forgiven

—feigning, faint—
all B wants
is to make it

through the day,
make it with that girl
make it period.

A self-unmade
man, he has
got his future

to drink about
& to
—how short—

SWINE©. Meat
market art—living high
on the hog

hamstrung.
ANIMATED PIG
100 PURE MEAT

TOP TEE—
this big wig
little pig going

whole hog
heaven.
Hot dog!—B

B Q on the block,
gone from the rooter
to the tooter—

That's all—Folks—she wrote.

37. Out Getting Ribs

Back in
blank
minutes—

cooking, really
putting his
foot in it—

charcoal on paper.

Pickled pig
knuckles
have nothing

on these drawings,
nothing left
on the bone—HUMERUS

ANTERIOR VIEW
13 VIEWS
OF THE SHOULDER

JOINT OPENED—
smoked
like a rib, a spliff

passed—out
of it, to lunch. Forget
cannibanalism,

this cannibis
so good it sticks
the ribs—rolling

papers. Go ask Eve™
& that snake
of a man

AN UNRSNBLE
FCSMILE
steak tartar

through his heart—
pass the SALT©
shaking, aimed

—a gun
or a bill-
board—menthol—

the Morton Girl
has kilt
more blk men

than gin, either
cotton or clear.
RIGHT HUMERUS

FRONT VIEW BACK
VIEW OUTER SIDE
INNER

Away in a mangy
manger
Baby Jesus®

surrounded by beef,
lamb, the little
ear drummer

boy—BACK VIEW
FEMALE PELVIS
PHALANGES.

HEAD OF
THE RADIUS
FOURTH LUMBAR—

Bacon grease gives
broth that fine
flavor NASAL

NASAL NOTCH
STYLOID PROCESS
doo rags doo wop

GREAT WIND OF SPHENOID
We sneak
bacon & CHKN—

LIFE EXEPECTANCY
OF THE AFRICAN
Open mouth—insert

111

FOOT LUNG HOT DOG.

Why save face
when you can
spend it?

SUBSTANTIA NIGRA
SUBSTANTIA NIGRA
THE RED NUCLEUS—

For once
Basquiat's got
enough

money to burn
—his walking papers—
taken the town

by storm—sold out
his show, pockets
chalk full

of a hundred bones.

38. Shadow Boxing

works on canvas

In those days I never had enough money to cover a whole canvas. I wouldn't be surprised if I died like a boxer, really broke, but somehow I doubt it.

—JEAN-MICHEL BASQUIAT
"Report from New York: The Graffiti Question"

SAINT JOE LOUIS
SURROUNDED BY SNAKES

BIP! SPLAT!
BOP!
EAST. The Harlem

HVYWT CHAMP
WORLD
taking

a whupping. DOES NOT
FIGURE
SOME EARLY LICK

MUST NOT YIELD.
One night only—
SCHH VS. SCH

SCHSCHMSCHM
SCHSCHM
SCHMELING, MAX—

Hindenberged
home, a hero.
Uber-

mensch.
©1936
KING

FEATURES
SYNDICATE—
Rematch

against Saint
Joe Louis,
the whole of Harlem

listening. All
or nothing.
1,000,000 YEN.

Y* BL*ST*D
SW*B
struck through,

crossed
out—combination,
jab, upper

hand. All the flags
of Harlem USA
raised

like fists.
Jubilee.
The Brown

Embalmer
in this corner
BOXED (x 3)

BOXEO

his gloves down.
CROWN.
Trainers round

his neck like towels
halo
hiss his cauliflower ear.

SUGAR RAY

1982, acrylic & oil paintstick
42 x 42 inches

No stretcher—

nailed instead
to the boards

of a pallet, kind
that forklifts

stored papers
—CONFIDENTIAL—

or crates cages
of fresh fruit—

ON HIS BACK
TO THE SVCKERPVNCH

OF HIS CHILDHOOD
FILES—

this black canvas can
barely hold SUGAR

RAY ROBINSON
his toothed

face, torso
outlined, crowned.

"That boy's sure
sweet as sugar."

Heavyweight,
feather, welter—

whatever
this weight

he's blue
as a bruise,

undertone of sky
traced beside

his clear chin—
winning streaks

of pale blue
in this here corner

where BSQT 83
used to be, covered

up like victory, names
on last year's trophy—

erased like Ray's given
name, traded

for a retired union card—
this Smith turned

Robinson—like Crusoe
—like Mr

Bojangles
whose routines

he copied in Hell's
Kitchen, in Harlem—

dancing the way Walker
became Ray—

sun, X, sting.

Just WHY do Europeans like Negroes from the States? Sugar Ray Robinson, who was treated like a King when touring Europe, offers this answer:

"Over there they aren't interested in your color, your background or pocketbook. All they want to know is 'What can you offer and whether you will be an asset to their city and country?' If the answers are all 'Yes,' then you'll score a clean K.O. with the people. They love us for what we are."

—*Brown* tabloid magazine
June 1954

39. B.O.

During the 60s a lot of people I knew seemed to think that underarm smell was attractive. They never seemed to be wearing anything washable. Everything always had to be dry-cleaned —the satins, the sewn-on mirrors, the velvets—the problem was that it never was dry-cleaned.

TUESDAY, 9 AUGUST 1983

Paige stayed overnight with Jean Michel in his dirty smelly loft downtown. How I know it smells is because Chris was there and said…there were crumpled-up hundred-dollar bills in the corner and bad b.o. all over and you step on paintings.

The day Jean Michel came over to exercise with me he made a point of saying that Paige had made it to work on time, so that's how he was letting me know. He'd thought that Paige was Jay's girlfriend, which she was at one point, but then he asked her out and she went.

And they had a date and this was the date—they rented a U-Haul and went out to Brooklyn to a black neighborhood and went to a White Castle and had eight hamburgers and then two people came in with big sticks and they thought they were going to kill them. You know, it was a "kooky date."

WEDNESDAY, 17 AUGUST 1983

Went down to meet Jean Michel and did a workout with him and Lidija (cab $5). And he has b.o. It's like Chris who also thinks it's sexy when you exercise to have b.o., but I want to say, it sure isn't. And all this b.o. has made me think about my life and how I'm not really missing anything great. I mean, I think of Paige having sex with Jean Michel and I think, how could she do it. I mean, what do you do, say some hint like, "Uh, gee, why don't we do something wild like take a shower together?"

WEDNESDAY, 5 OCTOBER 1983—NY—MILAN

Jean Michel Basquiat came by the office to work out with Lidija and I told him I was going to Milan and he said he'd go, too, that he'd meet us at the airport. Worked all afternoon till 4:30.

I hadn't thought Jean Michel would come, but while I was wait-
ing in line at the airport he appeared, he was just so nutty but
cute and adorable. He hadn't slept in four days, he said he was
going to watch me sleep. He had snot all over the place. He was
blowing his nose in paper bags. It was as bad as Christopher.
Paige has turned him into sort of a gentleman, though, because
now he's taking baths.

THURSDAY, 6 OCTOBER 1983—MILAN

Jean Michel came by and said he was depressed and was going
to kill himself and I laughed and said it was just because he
hadn't slept for four days, and then after a while of that he went
back to his room.

FRIDAY, 7 OCTOBER 1983—MILAN

Jean Michel came back and I got him to do artwork on plates so
we gave everyone a portrait on a plate. And it was glamorous and
the kids went off dancing and Jean Michel made a big play for
Joanna Carson who was in Milan.

TUESDAY, 11 OCTOBER 1983—PARIS—NEW YORK

When I got home to 66th Street I didn't shower because I knew
that if I did I'd never get to work. I was wearing *(laughs)*
"Essence of France"—b.o.

Worked till 7:00 or 7:30. Ronnie Cutrone came by and said that
he was in Milan when we were and that Jean Michel went off to
Madrid. Jean Michel's trying to get so famous so fast, and if it
works, he'll have it, I guess.

WEDNESDAY, 12 OCTOBER 1983

And Paige is really upset because Jean Michel hasn't called her.
He hasn't called us, either. She sells his paintings, she's been
doing that for a while. And he dropped Mary Boone—she took
50 percent, Paige only takes 10 percent. He's still with Bruno,
though, so that's how he'll still be shown. I told Paige that Jean
Michel was after Joanna Carson in Milan, and maybe I shouldn't
have. Paige said she might just forget him, that it had to be all or
nothing. But naturally people are people and a fool is a fool so no
matter what they say, they'll just go on being in love.

Jean Michel came by and I slapped him in the face. *(laughs)* I'm not kidding. Kind of hard. It shook him up a little. I told him, "How dare you dump us in Milan!" Benjamin put me up to it.

PHILOSOPHY

Good b.o. means good "box office." You can smell it from a mile away. The more you spell it out, the bigger the smell. And the bigger the smell, the more b.o. you get.

40. In Italian

a trip

The West Indian posed as a prize fighter and made quite a few lire letting much smaller and weaker Italian boxers knock him out, while the crowd roared at the prowess of Italy. No doubt, he is quite rich by now, this Negro, and is probably posing as an Ethiopian, and still getting knocked out.

—LANGSTON HUGHES
The Big Sea

THESIS   1983

Off the record, please—
Exhibit B
building up

his resistance—
"LUX LUCET IN TENEBRIS"
RED CROSS, PARKER

SOLO, BEGINNING OF—
getting a taste
of what's next—the fire

of time. IMPORTED MEAT.
Arsonist,
artist—a new lease

life. Search & destroy
deploying decoys
i.e. Trojan

Horse—CANINE
PRE MOLAR
SAME SIZE RIVER.

Crossed Rubicon
's cube, crossed
hisself holy—

MONA LISA
FALLING THE STAIRS
DOWN—

A
GOOD
PAINTING.

"PERFECT Δ
FROM EYES
TO CENTER

BREAST." Head
bobs on his chest
CLAY BUST

W/ THORNS—
a foreign needle
exchange student

enrolls this crash
& burn course. Europe
on $5 a day

or less. Drum
talk, smoke
signals—INVENT

ENEMIES.
For Immediate
Release Please Post—

Low Boy
In Junkie Paradise
obeying LEAPSICKNESS

THE LAW
OF LIQUIDS—
go to lowest

point, & stay.

FLASH IN VENICE

   Like lightening
SHAZAM!
he zigzags

across Europa—
speed of sound,
light, speed

in hand swallowed—
run so fast
won't sink

in water, can
alter the atoms
in body & thus

walk through walls
—outrun bullet—
faster human eye.

Worried he's a flash
in the pan, an art
test dummy—

Draw "Tippy"
Turtle & send
us—Sketch famous

Draw Me Head
using pencil or pen
—We will judge—

2. Do you enjoy art
   enough to want
   to improve?

3. Did you study in
grade school?
4. Other art training
5. How much devote
each week?

7. Other members family
artistic?

Like THOR
of North, found god
in a lightning rod—

a club—made his hair
grow. Now done
with blonde

he's moved on—fast
track—secret ID—
minus a mask

FALSE

ROMULUS + REMUS
saying uncle
uddering

under the she-wolf
—THEATER SEATS.
APHRODITE.

PERICLES. Perilous
road leads
him here—hunger

plan B on a crash
test diet—
delicious shakes

for breakfast lunch,
a sensible withdrawal
for dinner. Scars-

dale. Count
Chocula. BRUTUS AS
1ST CONSUL. Fiending—

B in need
of refreshdment
—the pillow mint

in the Ritz
—something to fill
his stocking

like coal. Black
Peter. Salt.
"PAX ROMANA"—

B in the head
losing his
—steers

that porcelain
bus—SANITIZED—
Do Not Disturb.

Et tu, Rufus?

TRUE FALSE
—his technicolor
yawn his just

say ahh
—wrecks his hotel
like a ship—

sunk. ROME IS SACKED
BY GOTHS.
—Does that Dick

Gregory dance
striking hunger.
—Does portraits

on a plate
then gives
them away—ANDY

WARHOL
"BOY GENIUS"
—PABLO PICASSO

(the eyes)
—FRANZ KLINE
with splashes

of black across
the fine white
chinette (all owned

by the Warhol Estate).
ALEXANDER
THE GREAT (x 2)—

B in the john
just saying
No—FALSO—

BARBARIAN
INVADER FOR FIRST TIME
SEES ROME

THE ITALIAN VERSION OF POPEYE
HAS NO PORK IN HIS DIET

Anchors
on the insides
of his arms

aweigh—
inked on
by needle

drill syringe—
wants spinach
without oink

greens minus
ham hocks
prosciutto

pepperoni
HOO
HOO HOOVES—

can lid flipped
open like Sailor Man's
one good looker

ahoy matey—
Sweepea, Olive
Oyl, a corn

cob pipe
puffing away
in his mouth

choo choo—
~~BUM~~ BUM
EAR—BRACCO

DI FERRE—
Bluto blottoed
ko'd, Wimpy

wanting a nickel
Will gladly pay
you Tuesday

for a hamburger today—
FOUR BIG
100% PERCENT

He's strong
to the finish
cause he eats

him spinach—
able, again,
to save the day

POPEYE VERSUS THE NAZIS

KRYPTON.
A PLACE
TO MOVE

NEGROS.
COLORED PEOPLE.
FATS TRYING

TO ESCAPE
THE SKIN.
CADIUM. YELLOW

LIGAMENT.
TEN PER
CENT.

(PECHO.)
FAMOUS NEGRO
ATHLETES NO.

#47—
SPECIMEN.
BROOKLYN

DODGERS.
ELBOW
ELBOW BUST

OF A NEGRO—
UPPER TORSO.
(ERROR.)

ESOPHAGUS.
INTFERIORITY   PLEX.
NECK. SCHIZOPHRENIC.

FATS TRYING TO ESCAPE
THE SKIN.
ULTRA HIGH

FUREQUENCY.
P. ROEBSON.
ACTION COMICS

AT HIS PRIME
—DYNAMIC—
CRISPUS ATTUCKS

HIGH. PREE
1951-1953
"CHEROKEE"

SWALLOWS IODINE?
¿POW?
BRUNO BELIEVE

SPINACH
IS POISON.
KRYPTONITE.

JIMMY OLSEN.
BERLIN 1936—
JESSE OWEN

CATHARSIS

What all
he's missing
—SPLEEN

LIVER LEFT
PAW. B been
losing it—fold

perforated line & tear
—SUICIDE ATTEMPT—
why not just

jump ship, swim
for it? He's tired
of this feeling

127

of feeling
a thing. THUMB.
ARM.

RADIUM. He's in
the dark, glowing
glowers. How

old it's grown—
IL MANO—
the fist made

of his THROAT.
His neck's guillotine
fit—perfect—

strains in the Sistine
Chapel to see
the gap between

God's hand
& human—torn
from his side.

SWALLOWS IODINE
Yardbird does,
not the first time

he inked his insides
& felt the dye
spread—cast—that feeling

again—DIZZY
ATMOSPHERE
ALL THE THINGS YOU ARE—

suffers
niggeritis—African
sleeping sickness

~~FIRST DRAFT~~
FINISHED
PRODUCT—may

cause drowsiness.
Doses, dozes—FORTEZZA—
take 2 & call

it mourning.

41. Onion Gum   { 1983 }

ONION GUM
MAKES YOUR
MOUTH TASTE

LIKE ONIONS
ONION GUM
MAKES YR MOUTH

TASTE LIKE ONIONS
INGREDIENTS:
ENRICHED FLOUR

Bunion gum makes
your mouth taste
like bunions

Bunion gum makes
your feet taste
like bunions

NIACIN, REDUCED IRON
Union gum
makes your

mouth taste
like Lincoln
Union gum

makes your mouth
head south
RIBOFLAVIN

engine engine
Injun gum
makes your

mouth taste
tobacco Injun
gum makes your

mouth taste
lottery
union gun

onion gun
Ink gum
makes your

mouth taste
calamari
Ink gum

makes your
mouth turn
negro

cuttle gum
colored gum
Bubble gum

makes yr mouth
pink & sore
Bubble gum

makes yr mouth
blow sugar
über gum

bazooka gum
THIAMINE
MONONITRATE

MADE IN JAPAN©
Redhot gum
makes yr mouth

taste like pepper
Redhot gum
makes yr mouth

taste like love
SNAKE
SERPENT

"HARMLSS"
ur-gum
anti-gum

ONION GUM
MAKES YR MOUTH
TASTE LIKE

ONIONS ONION
GUM MAKES
YOUR MOUTH

TASTE LK ONIONS

42. Wine of Babylon   { 1984 }

Mr T pity
the fool who
wears his red

suit to the White
House—no bus
boy—just Mr T

duded up as Santie
Claus, arms around
the First Lady—

fine china. Linens.
Silver
service. Gold

around his neck
—not noosed—he say
the weight of slave

chains. South
African mines.
GLOBAL/INDUSTRIAL.

BOILING POINT OF WATER.

Divestment,
diversions, division
of labor. No Secretary

of State—just mohawked
Mr T, challenger
to Rocky Balboa,

taking/trading
blows. UHNN.
Eye

of Tiger. EYE
OF HORUS
—PROTECTION

—HEALING
He pilot
the helicopter

to drop on the enemy
city a bomb. A-Team.
Special agent

secret. SOW'S EAR/
SILK PURSE.
NON-TOXIC

on a toy elephant.
Gilded, gelding—
No animals

harmed in the making—
a cheshire cat, striped
black, disappearing

till only the grin remains—

43. Battle Royale

may the best man win

HG: *I heard you'd been spreading a rumor that you wanted to have a boxing match with Julian Schnabel.*
JMB: This was before I'd ever met him. And one day he came into Annina's gallery. And I asked him if he wanted to spar.

HG. *He's pretty strong.*
JMB: Oh yeah, I thought so. But I figured even if I lost, I couldn't look bad.

—*Making It New*

MUHAMMAD ALI BY ANDY WARHOL

*1977, acrylic & silkscreen ink
on canvas*

Knockout—
looker, loose

talker. Your
mama.

Colorful
in Warhol

's red wash—
fists up

like pre-fight
predictions—

Ali fingers what rounds
his opponents

will go down.
Who knew when they paid

*to see a fight
they'd see the launching*

of a colored satellite!
Battled Frazier—

that ugly gorilla
(whose grandmother

had blond hair
down to here) enough

times to shorten both
their lives. Hospitalized.

Lips fat
as their bank

as bacon. Swelled
heads. His skin

tone brown,
even, mixed

by an assistant—
still the lips

are his, not stock
or air-

brushed. Full.
No smile.

CASSIUS CLAY BY BASQUIAT

*1982, acrylic & oil paintstick
on canvas*

*I'm pretty!
I shook up*

the world! Clay shouts
to the announcer

after trouncing
Sonny Liston—

the next day he
will turn Ali.

Butterfly,
bee—none stung

or swole carpet-red
as the paint B covered

this canvas, drawing
blood—not even Cassius

called out his name.
Refusing to recognize

Allah—like Terrell
or fool Floyd Patterson—

will get you a new haircut,
whether you want one

or not. How
he hounds

Liston, waving
his prize belt—

a noose for Sonny's ex-
con neck. Petty crook.

Ali just bout serves
time himself

—title stripped
like paint

—Army taking away
his right to fight

when he won't fight
them Viet Cong

who've done him
nothing wrong.

Houston, we gots
a problem—will not

bow or stand
when his no-longer-

name the Draft
Board calls. Lords

over Liston
—*Get up, you bum!*

—who will fall to a phantom
punch 1st rd, forget

to get up. (Died,
Liston did, five

years later, in Vegas,
the needle in

his arm, the neon.)
Ali, now he could hit you

into next year—
but apart from the flogging,

his flaunting, were the taunts
challengers heard ringing

*Uncle Tom! Come on
Come on White America!*

even above the ten count
& crowd—his undented smile—

that smarts still.

The Americans should be protesting
to save the young boys
Instead of wasting time protesting
the Concorde's noise.
The Concorde is the greatest thing
in the history of mankind.
When headed in the right direction
it outruns the sunshine.
The Americans left England years ago
in order to be free
So they should remember that the
people made the Concorde
Out of the roots of their tree.

—MUHAMMAD ALI
Andy Warhol's Exposures

44. First Class   { 1983 }

Untitled, *oilstick on paper*
50 x 96 1/2 in.

Lands
from the Concorde
unable to catch

a cab—REPLACEMENT—
MILK
BONES—SPIN

AL TAP.
10 MILES
FIVE MILES

20 MILES—
rainsoaked Basquiat
hails in vain—

COWBOY HAT
WAGE CONCESSION
CHINESE LABOR.

MICE. LARGE DOG.
UPPER TEETH AND JAW.
Hotshot

hopping mad, gracious
furious—
MOLTEN METAL

SOUTH. SOUTH.
UN BOMBERO
ERROR

ADMIRAL BYRD.
Walking
homeward, still waving

down the yellow
the checkered cars—
READING RAILROAD

SHORT
LINE RAILROAD
B & O—

COAL. Dreadlocks
drenched—A REAL
CHAMPION—but no one

stops.
Gives up.
rodent festival

union
pacific co.—
paint-wet Basquiat

hoofing it, catching
the subway
like a cold.

best remembered
as jimmy olsen.
Superman or super-

intendent—
1. MANUAL
2. ELECTRIC

don't matter
how much you makes,
what cut

your hair—
degraded Basquiat
has grown

used to this,
ingrate Basquiat
never—

~~the usual~~
~~horror~~
~~story~~

baseballs
made in
haiti—

big man in a blue suit
and the end
of the 20th century.

Side **3** Takes

DISC **1**: ZYDECO

45. HOLLYWOOD AFRICANS. 1983.
46. COKE® (THE REAL THING).
47. CROWN.
48. SELF-PORTRAIT AS A HEEL. 1982.
49. SELF-PORTRAIT AS A HEEL, PART TWO. 1982.
50. FAMOUS NEGRO ATHLETE.
51. GOLD ALLOY POWDER.
52. DISCOGRAPHY ONE: made from original masters
53. HORN PLAYERS.
54. HISTOIRE DE PEUPLE NOIR (DETAIL).
55. UNDISCOVERED GENIUS OF THE MISSISSIPPI DELTA.
56. REVISED UNDISCOVERED GENIUS OF THE MISSISSIPPI DELTA.
57. COLOR.
58. FAKE/NEW. 1983.

59. KING ZULU
60. SKIN HEAD WIG.
61. FROGMEN. 1983.
62. TOXIC. 1984.
63. DISCOGRAPHY TWO: digitally remastered
64. BLACK MAN, THE. 1984.
65. ZYDECO. 1984.
66. LANGSTON HUGHES. 1983.
67. LOGO.

{ All Colored Cast }

The most expensive habit in the world is celluloid, not heroin, and I need a fix every two years.

—STEVEN SPIELBERG
Wired

45. Hollywood Africans   { 1983 }

Basquiat paints

the town. PAW.
BWANA. SEVEN
STARS. Night

life—star-struck
Basquiat's arrived,
brought Toxic

& Rammellzee along
for the ride. Our trio
stomping new

ground—shaky,
kept. *Hills,*
that is—black

gold, Texas tea—
out west
Basquiat burns

his canvas ochre,
this trinity thin
as their ties. *Hip*

hop hippity hop—
Sunset Blvd
Walk of the Stars,

streets stretched
like limos. B
at last in the black,

dines out at Mr. Chow's.
IDI AMIN. 200 YEN.
Put it on his tab—

trading meals
for canvases free
loaded with msgs,

HERO-ISM.
TOBACCO in purple,
palimpsest. Toxic

& RMLZ cool, eyes
shaded by goggles,
hats with ZS. Snores

ville. GANGSTERISM.
SELF-PORTRAIT
AS A HEEL #3. Hail,

hail, the gang's all
heels—no winners
or winters, just

wanderlust
amongst Oscars®
& MOVIE STAR

FOOTPRINTS
like an astronaut's.
Rock rock planet rock

don't stop—POP
CORN—SUGAR
CANE. Academy

Mammy Award
& another for Butler,
Rhett—To the moon

Jemima—PAW—
Basquiat rockets
NEW!—hands pressed

fresh into pavement,
permanent as a rap
sheet, booked.

Jean-Michel called at 8:00 in the morning and we philosophized. He got scared reading the Belushi book. I told him that if he wanted to become a legend, too, he should just keep going on like he was. But actually if he's even on the phone talking to me, he's okay. And the phone calls from pay phones are now $.25. I'm just not going to make calls anymore.

—*Andy Warhol Diaries*
MONDAY, JULY 2, 1984

48. Self-Portrait as a Heel   { 1982 }

Cheeseburger
Cheeseburger
No Coke—

Pepsi. Belushi
burns his candle
both ends

against the middle.
Midnight
oil. Commits

hari kari—knocking
em dead. Live
wire—Belushi

getting big
ACE COMB©
game for some

black beauties
to pop, keep
him up. *Food*

fight! Face first
in white
powder—cream

or cocaine, code
name *watermelon*—
riding

high. *But*
noooooo! Kamikaze
Belushi belly

flops—*1941*—
has got to score
another hit, drag

himself off the cutting
room floor.
Numbers

across his chest
like reels.
Speed

balls along—*on*
a mission
from God

the Blues Bros.
trying to save
the convent, their souls.

You better think
—think—think about
what you're trying—

Queen Aretha
croons at the diner
in an apron

& house-shoes—
James Brown
the preacher—Ray

Charles shining, all-seeing.
UNIVERSAL.
They even catch Cab

Calloway
get him to run
through Minnie

the Moocher, she was
a low
down hoochie

coocher—Belushi
launching another
routine, back flips

an encore. It's never
like the movies, baby—
no cab checkered

as the past to pick
you up—instead it's daylight
& there's no rain—

only B in the sewer

on his knees, don't
shoot, he's sorry,
don't want to die, please

save his
hide—*hi de*
hi de hi de ho—

Who can resist
those eyes? A last
kiss. Name etched

to his knuckles
like a stone. In blueface
beside his Brother, both

decked in undertaker
black, sunglasses, the mask
of a mourner—

49. Self Portrait as a Heel, Part Two

Brown
boy at the bar
downing tin

& gonics—
mixes his volatile
cocktail—one part

pain, the other
champ—
this bubblubling

in his nose—feeling
Live & Smokin'
like Rich-

ard Pryor, a stand-up
guy—he's been placed
on seven

second delay (just
in case he bleeps)
& not even known it

like the time Pryor was host

—no supper
no last request—
live it's Saturday Nite.

He's only a guest.
Or samurai busboy, worse.
Your mamasan.

He spills like news
his drink, douses
hisself generous as Pryor

the brush fire
—Holy Moses, it speaks—
running down the street

racing like poor Jesse
Owens, late
in life, in the hippodrome

—an exhibition—
versus
some heartwormed horse

50. Famous Negro Athlete

B anomaly—
anomaly he be—
caught between

a hock
& a hard race—
From the peak

you can almost see

the far
side of the river
Lights stretch

out suburban
satisfied
Black is this

season in
It goes
with everythin—

They know not
who he is because
he is not like

what ever they know—

Lashed
to the mast
the hero rides

past, ignoring
the sirens
steering by stars

& desire
Only he can hear
The others' ears

stuffed w/ cotton
so's not to listen—
what leads us

into the water we
inhale
as if air, smiling

whiles we die—
Bliss is this—
Is not his

luxury, no matter
how heavy
his pockets, how full

No one will let
Gentleman Jack
Johns'n board this Titanic—

O how the ship will rock
when it meets
that giant block

of ice—doing
the Eagle Rock—
it's not what

you can see
—the white—
that kills, but what you cannot

51. Gold Alloy Powder

Angel star gold

whatever they call
the dust, he must
get him some—

like the Gold
Dust twins
he's siamese

almost, joined
at the arm & grin
by need—

trying to scrub
his skin off.
Like Ole Blues

Eyes in *Man
Golden Arm*
he can play

no more the drums
or pretend
this monkey

ain't his. Cut—
they call him Dealer
cause he can send

the cards
like race
spinning, spades

ace hole.

Gotta score
to deal all
night—tomorrow

he's got this break
to play
with the big

boys band,
& here he is
messing it up

once more, stoned
like a bible sinner
at the Safari Club.

Even his lady
in waiting (not wife)
don't want him

at the Safari Club.
Neon need.
Time to rewind

dust angel golden

to when, back
on the street, clean
again, he walked

into the place,
the stilted city
sets, & ordered

a drink
while his connection
made the one-

legged beggar
dance laugh dance
for two bits of change.

52. Discography One

*made from original
masters*

SATCHMO

SIDE A—
the face handled
careful, black

wax grooves
going round
in an endless

endless grin—
King Louie
Armstrong

blowing like no
tomorrow.
Oooh hoo

*I wanna be
like you-who—*
Pops wipes his brow

with a kerchief
as if cleaning
a needle, a skipping

dusty LP.
*An ape like me
would love to be*

human too.
SIDE B—
his bull

horn muffled,
sounding fog—
labels spun

too fast
to read. Heebie
Jeebies. *Is*

*you is or is
you ain't—*
Satchelmouth

Old Scratch,
between the devil
& the deep

blue sea—his Hot Fives
scat, out-play
Beezlebub on a good

day—two horns
twisted
up out his hair—

NOW'S THE TIME

Cross the room it looks
like a giant
pupil or dark nipple

—a black bullseye—

a tree sliced sidelong
trunk
telling age, all—

"NOW'S THE TIME"
underline
PRKR

the blacked wood
warped, an eclipse
a 78 —don't stare

directly—up close
see the seam
stitching together

the halves—the have
nots—one small step
for man, one Giant

Step for sax—
captured
by wax—Bird

sears, soars
splitting
his reeds—

STARDUST

Lady sings
the blues
the reds, whatever

she can find—
short
changed, a chord—

God bless
the child
that's got his own

& won't mind
sharing some—
"BILLIES BOUNCE"

"BILLIES BOUNCE"
Miss Holiday's up
on four counts

of possession, three-
fifths, the law
—locked up—

licked—the salt
the boot—refused
a chance to belt

tunes in the clubs—
ex-con. Man,
she got it

bad—Brother
can you spare
a dime

bag? MEANDERING
WARMING UP
A RIFF—

she's all scat,
waxing—
SIDE A

SIDE B
OOH
SHOO DE

OBEE—
detoxed, thawed
in time

for Thanksgiving—live
as ammo, smoking
—NOV. 26 1945—

Day cold as turkey—

LESTER YELLOW

Sax held side-
ways—like South
America upside

down, mouth-
piece Peru—
playing up

beat, on
the one—pork-
pie hat cymbal-flat—

wearing it out—

Les hits it first
like Matthew
Henson at the North

Pole. *N.B.:* There
're more penguins off
the coast of Brazil

than swim in the arctic.
Lady, let's call
him Prez

let him lead us—

mush
mush hyah
—N E E N A H—

the way Henson
became Inuit.
Cool. His heart

an ig-
loo, warm
inside. State

of the Union,
Bering Strait,
T*NY HARM*N*CA—

Saxophone a flag
blowing—
perched on top

of this world
slicked in ice—
Cf..:

Some cultures have

up to 27 diff.
words
for white

MAX ROACH

What had happened was—

He woke up one day
with the bug—
six-armed, slick—antennae

two sticks to beat things with

His ears gone
inner, got his behind
behind a kit

& began to bang, *tukuh*

tukuduh, scraping
the snares, barn-
storming fleabit motels

Scraps of food & sex

Only when the lights shut
off do Roach
come out & play

Seems forever he'll be here

Post-nukelar, klook mopped,
thermodynamic—
La Cucaracha taught

them beetles a thing

about survival, dropping
bombs—digging
in—a scarab buried

longside pharaoh's amber skin

53. Horn Players

Woodshedding
done, we cut
our chops—pork

oak—took
our ax
to town—task—

"Cherokee"

turned KO KO—
RECORDED
NEW YORK WOR

STUDIOS—
Max, Miles
Dizzy

"Tea for Two"

We left off
the King
Cotton, Swing—

ANGLOSAXAPHONE—
We shot the shit
—the breeze—up

town, down

beat—wind—
PREE
1951-1953

We earned them cows,
lines,
found that soft

spot—CHARLIE
PARKER'S PLASTIC
SAX

"BIRD SIPPING CHAMPAGNE"

& split—spilt
the beans—red,
baked, blackeyed luck—

54. Histoire de Peuple Noir (Detail)

three panels, exposed wood supports,
68 x 141 in. overall

SICKLE. The Pharoah's
boat curving
EL GRAN ESPECTACULO—

headed east. NUBA.
MUJER. Arrows
guiding us, oars.

Anansi in pink.
It's all Greek to
MEMPHIS—

HEMLOCK. ESCLAVE.
The eye
of the storm, A DOG

GUARDING
THE PHAROH.
AMENOPATHS. THEBES.

TENNESSEE.

55. Undiscovered Genius
   of the Mississippi Delta

From Hazlehurst
        Mississip's
Most Diversified County

From Hazlehurst
        Center of Copiah
Down Hazlehurst way

He split like
        a boll weevil
wanting no part of no

COTTON
        ORIGIN OF
P. 4

picking only
        that guitar of his
cross every jook

in the Delta—
        music his alpha
& omega—his Satan—he slid easy

like the neck of a guitar
        IV: THE DEEP
SOUTH 1912-1936-1951

Only thing easier
        was picking women
NEGROES

NEGROES
        UDDER
NEGROES —

Find you the ugliest
        pug ugliest
woman in town

Love her & she'll
        treat you swell—
Awww wouldn't we

have a time babe—
        He made a killin
each town he played

shacking up
        with a lady
who'd get him

three squares, hot—
        A DIET RICH
IN PORK PRODUCTS—

THE "COW" IS
        A REGISTERED
TRADEMARK—

then ramblin on.
        FIG 23: cigarette low
from his lip—

Married secretly
        & didn't much care
whether a lady

be spoken for—
        Even better
if she was—

no strings.
        He blurred them chords
He wed the underworld

blessed by corn
        NO MORE—
MULES—

& crossroads.
        He'd played
till nothing was dry

no throat nor eye—NEITHER
        SWORD NOR SPAR
DISPERSED INTO THE FOUR

CORNERS OF THE EARTH—
        got chased
out of town more times

than he could count—
        A. SICKLES
B. MATTOCKS

C. FORKS
D. AXES
Hear them dogs closing like a train.

Each lady knew
he was singing
for her

Every hand knew
it was his gal who
that Johnson boy was crooning to—

Played his home
town, flirting
with trouble, wife

of the jook joint's owner—
sipped bottles unsealed
thinking them kisses

She winked & he winced
He took him another
swig, kept on singing—

MISSISSIPPI
MISSISSIPPI
MISSISSIPPI MISSISSIPPI

SLAVE SHIP—
the poison's sicksweet clutch.
EL RATON.

Hellhounds—heels—

Soon couldn't stand
stopped his number
to stumble outside

1. EAST
2. WEST
3. NORTH

ground spinning
like a cotton gin.
PER LB. 49¢

NOSTRILS
JAW TEETH
LARYNX

SIDE VIEW.
1. Place of Death
Greenwood (Outside)

2. Full Name
    Robert L. Johnson
3. Sex   *M*

4. Color or Race
    B
5. Single, Married, Widowed,

or Divorced (write
    the word)
Single

7. Years
    26—
the dirt deep around

Three Forks,
    the jook clearing out
Serves him right

Sho you're right
    18. Burial,
Cremation, or Removal

19. Undertaker
    Family.
His strong

heart held on
    four days before
the poison colded him—

in his chest
    a train
derailing—

before the blues caught
    up & hounded him
MARK TWAIN

MARK TWAIN
    MARK TWAIN
TWAIN

out his cotton pickin mind.

56. Revised Undiscovered Genius of the Mississippi Delta

Struggles
   up the stairs for days
     or they carry him

to the landing—once
   inside, he can't quite
     walk around his own

show at the Center
   for the New South—
     born into

slavery, bred
   a sharecropper,
     he spent all

his uncounted years behind
   mules who wouldn't move—
     He's sullin,

don't budge. Stayed
   put, laboring
     beneath the Belt

Black as a Bible.
   He storks
     across his exhibit

a hothouse flower
   or ostrich, saying
     little, slow steps

stilting the room.
   Walls teem
     with his silhouettes,

giant dogs.
   CATFISH.
     The ripe

cardboard canvases
   sun-browned
     primed

beside the old Coke
   machine.
     He seen

it all, enough—
      time
            to return

to his corner
      —the market—
            the young boys

who set a spell
      while he works—the white
            youth who stops by

& takes away
      Mr Traylor's art
            in exchange

for fresh cardboard,
      some oils.
            ~~CATFISH~~.

Thanks kindly. Traylor still
      prefers the old backings
            from men's shirts, the kind

the dead wear, across the street
      in the funeral parlor—
            where he, on his flat

pallet, sleeps.

57. Color

YELLOW OCHRE

high yaller
yaller
pink-toes

mustard seed
punkin seed
honey

coppered
lemon-colored
olive

BURNT UMBER

high brown
cocoa
chestnut

coffee-colored
nut brown
maroon

vaseline brown
sealskin
low brown

PAYNE'S GRAY

charcoal
ebony black
eight-rock

eight-ball
inky dink
dark black

low black
lam black
damn black

blue

58. Fake/New { 1983 }

FAKE

The colors
too timid
The nose not solid

or broad enough
MONO MONO
TORSO

This hair's
not right,
too straight

The skull
a copy, an x-ray
of another

work from that year
CUPULA CUPULA
This shade far

too tame, even
pastel
200 YEN

SOL SOL SABIO
Doesn't take
no expert it's clear

this isn't his hand

NEW

His E's float
His E is a ladder
His O's do not meet

No one does
2's like his
THE REAL

LEONARDO DA VINCI
1594-1475
Note this pure yellow

placed, unafraid,
dead center
His teeth show, bare

His I's are straight
His eyes never close,
roll like R's, dice

His B's 13's!

59. King Zulu

Louis Armstrong, also known as Satch or Satchmo, for Satchelmouth, erstwhile Dippermouth, wearing the mask of the King of the Zulus in the Mardi Gras parade, New Orleans, 1949. Many civil rights spokesmen, for all their professed pride in their black African heritage, were downright scandalized when the long-since-renowned Armstrong declared that being chosen for such a role was the fulfillment of a lifelong dream. But perhaps they confused the ritual role of the Zulu King of Mardi Gras with that of minstrel entertainer. In any case they seem to have over-looked the fact (as a home-town boy would not) that the specific traditional ritual function of the outrageous costume and conduct of the King of the Zulus is to ridicule the whole idea of Mardi Gras and the Lenten Season.

—ALBERT MURRAY
Stomping the Blues

NATIVE CARRYING SOME GUNS,
BIBLES, AMORITES ON SAFARI

He love this world
with its overworked
mercies, its igloos

& the not-so-
insignificant
salaries—POACHERS

PROVISIONS
MISSIONARIES. He done
paid, full,

for the rain-sweated
streets—TUSKS GOD KIN—
these tropics,

his jungled head
of hair. Some bad
vines. I WON'T EVEN

MENTION GOLD.
(ORO). So, tough guy,
lessee what you got:

ten fingers counting
thumbs, a leg
over everyone—ROYAL

SALT INC ©—
& a million
midnights heavy as he

maybe can carry.

TOBACCO VERSUS RED CHIEF

He has remained
on bartime—borrowed—set
just ahead

in order to shut
up early—Sorry
Kemosabe, we're close—last

call, mohican. Maroon.
Make that
a double—lines

them up & knocks
them down. What's left
to want? We aren't—

he's got it all
figured out—How—
his problems fire-

water to walk—

JIM CROW

He need remedy
—MISSISSIPPI—is on
the edge—cutting—

has got to tame
take it off like a mask
or a prom

dress. Quick. Hopeless.
He's just
cause, a 24-hour pharmacy

he be—what else
to say? Swaying,
no use denying

what his body
craves—the beast
of his back—hunched

begging. WARNING:
Content
Under Pressure—

O the aisles
& aisles of his drugstore
mind—pain

relievers, cheap sun-
glasses, flesh
colored band-aids & Easter

candy overstock
he wants to ingest, fill his form
with—aerosal spray

Do Not Store Near Flame
to keep what's bug-
ging him away—

These milkshaking
counters—Woolworth—he once
could not, down south,

have sat & ordered up
a hot plate
of crow to eat—

LENT

Every day is Lent.
Each day he
giving up

something—meat,
smoke, smack-
crackle-pop—

holding out & forth
for his health.
Every day he gives away

175

hundreds
to the homeless guy washing
his cabby's window—

Keep the change
to whoever sold
him cigarettes. Each day

is Fat Tuesday, celebrating
something, or the things
that haven't killed us

yet. Each day
is Lent. Each day
giving in

to the skin with its pores
pouring out sweat
lust vomit—every day

he quits. Every day
repents, gives hisself
a second

chance, or given
—like a shotgun bride
wearing white—away.

60. Skin Head Wig   { 1982-83 }

So we are walking
And the dead
   And the dead

down Haight
Street, looking
   And the dead

for the day
for nothing particular—
Beneath concrete

the beach!
someone's written
under our feet—

the dunes long gone
from mixed
marriages to shops

selling the Summer
of Love, vintage duds
   And the dead

On the corner
some sidewalk
sale, junk—

a victrola
WORKS
the owner doesn't really

want to part with
PURE
ALL BEEF

piles of old
Playboys, dogged,
Miss April missing

   And the dead—
COMIC CODE
AUTHORITY

NO. 33—
Among Men
at Work & The Police

we find The Offs
album, cover
chalk on black

board—THE FINAL
BATATTLE
SMOKE

BOMB—recognize
your hand Basquiat
your halo

IBID.
IBID.
your white triangles—

No one believes
it's you
    And the dead

No one buys
you're here
on some punk's

sidewalk—
MOST PEOPLE TRY
TO GROW

HAIR THIS IS JUST
THE OPPISIT—
We pay

the skinhead
two bones
for the record—

MADE OF FLESH
TONED LATEX
WILL FIT—

Old Glory
tattooed to his arm,
boots laced

like stitches
to his knee,
an oxblood amputee

FOR THE EXECUTIVE
WHAT WOULD LIKE
TO CHANE

HIS APPEARANCE—
Turning the album
over we see

a man with a gun-
tattoo aimed
at his head

past
your name
      And the dead

And the dead—

61. Frogmen   { 1983 }

You big
lipped, good
for nothing,

coffee cooling
belching
full of bullfrog

thinks he's a prince—

bow-legged
flat-footed
SKIN HEAD WIG

green, yella,
legs too skinny
even for a meal—

tadpole
tail-chaser,
can't-decide-whether

you're under

water or above—
you worry wart-
hog-road-food

you witches brew
MUSEUM GUARDS
primitive artiste

who put the *you* in ugly—

you toady
footstool
lily-white-pad

sub-human sub-
marine—POLIZIA
TWO-PLY

TWO-PLY,
you bleepety
bleep

blankety blank

BROKEN STONE TIME
you thing caught
in the throat

whose name must
mean mud
you swamp-dweller

sludge-sucker
go back
go head & croak

62. Toxic   { 1984 }

CENTS in his
mouth like a scare-
crow stuffed

with news
print—a blanket
of words behind

him, infected,
undetected—hands
raised, braised

brown as turkey
legs. SMOKE
BOMB. SOUP

TO NUTS.
FIG 21—
EGG. Snake.

THAT EGG.
"BOY IT'S SURE
HOT HERE"—Bugs

Bunny, his goose
cooked over carrots—
GOLD. UNISON (INTRO)

all together now—
COMPOSED
TRUMPET SAX

(IMPROVED)—
his blue pork-
pie hat

a trumpet
muffler—
squealer. MILES

DAVIS. GREGOR
MENDEL INVENTOR
OF X-RAY—

blowing down trom-
bones. Half
lives. Old school.

Head spun—
an electron,
popping

locking, anti-
matter. Eureka!
DR RADIUM

turning lead
paint to oil,
gold

standard. Agent
orange.
Noble gas,

neon. Change
in his mouth
like a piggy bank

back, bills
piling up,
a beggar's dead

presidents
littering a hat—
VEHEMENT ALLEY CATS

GARBED A LA
KLU LUX KLAN PLAN
TO TORTURE THE—

notify next
of kin, a sign
on the doors

spare
our first born.
Hands raised—

a saint
or a sinner, holy
rolling.

Snake eyes.
Dice kissed
for luck—

"PORKY'S PIG FEAT"
RACKATEER RABBIT—
C'mon bones

baby needs
new shoes.
Just wave your hands

in the air!
Arms raised
in praise

or a stick up—
nobody moves
nobody hurt.

Around his cop-
colored, hip
hop top

hat, the halo
a cameo—
ODOURS OF PUNT.

LACK
OWDER
FROM AESOP'S

ER   AND HIS CAT"—
blown up—
POOF—a hit

record, a vinyl
spill—
gone platinum.

INDUSTRY©.
I'm the King
of Rock

there is none higher—
a silent
canary down

a mine.
Drunk off
Molotov

cocktails—
moonshine. White
lightning. Acid

rain. 40 ounces
& a mule—
prescription,

placebo, he's out
to score
a fifth

of prevention,
a pound
of flesh. Antidote

anodyne—CENTS
in his mouth
like God's

unsaid name in a golem's—

63. Discography Two

digitally remastered

JAZZ   1986

PER
PER
PERHAPS

NOT K"©

HUN 1 DUSK
HUN ÁN—DIM: DUSKY
HUNHUANG— "PALE YELLOW"

EINSTEINIUM

MARMADUKE
MAMADU
STEEPLECHASE—

CHARLIE PARKER REEBOPPERS

GUANO
FUEGO
"A IMAGE OF VICE"

7. FOR SUPPLYING DEAL
   IMPORTATION FLANDERS
   IMPROVEMENT OF LAND

   BREEDING HORSES

   50¢ PIECE

   FEDERAL RESERVE NOTE

   DIAGRAM
   OF THE NAVAL
   STRUCTURE

   OF A FIFTY
   CENT PIECE—
   RT EXCELLENCE

   MARCUS GARVEY

INDUSTRY
MOTOR AREA MEDULLA
CERBRUM

DR FRANCIOS DUVALIER
ALIAS "PAPA DOC"
SALT   HE AK

THE ARK

THE ARK WAS 300
CUBITS LONG

<------------------------------------>

MADE MOSTLY OF
WOOD AND PITCH©
11. PASTEURIZED

12. HOMOGENIZED
US OCCUPATION OF HAITI
ENDS 1936

TEN PERCENT
200 VOLT
P*R C*PITA—

BACK TO AFRICA
BCK TO ARIA
BXACK TO AFICA

BANK OF JAMAICA

QUALITY

POSTOAKOES
REST IN PEACE WHO TRUST?
WARM AIR FRONT

MASS SLUMS
CUTTHROATS
DUST BOWL

IDAHO
PUBLIC GHETTO
RIBS PORK

187

POPCORN
PER CAPITA
WHY VERSUS ROME.

QUALITY?
POLKA DOTS
IN PORT AU

PRINCE HAITI
PROPH E IES 59¢
GUILTY

200 BEATS PER MIN
E PLURIBUS
PILGRAMAGES

THIEVES
FROM THE MAYFLOWER
DISNEY©

1. STATUES
2. VENUES
JAMES VANDERZEE

POTATOES
CORN WHEAT
THE COTTON INDUSTRY

OF NINETEEN
THIRTY EIGHT
SHO'NUFF

JIFFY POP
DISPOMANIA
BANG POW

CRACK

PISCINE VS. THE BEST HOTELS

CHARLES 1: THE BALD
CHARLE 2: THE FAT
        3: THE SIMPLE—

AM
AN
AND

BLEACHERS
AT A BULLL
RING COLLAPSE.

ACK
       AVE
LOIN. THIGH.

SORTIE
SUR LE
TAPIS—

       AIR
ARK
   ART ACE

LAC D'ARGENT
BALD FAT
SIMPLE BURNED

MAYAN BOOKS.
FIRST CARTOON
(COLORED).

OLD BLACK
LADY SEWING
QUILT—

      JOHN
      LUTHER JONES
      RACING CAR HURLED

      INTO GRANDSTAND
      83 KILLLED.
      (HOI POLLOI—

EEP   ASH
AW
ANG

      DIES WITH
      HAND ON
      BRAKE

BLACK   1986

   MOO
RIP
PT. ONE

"LOUIS ARMSTONG"©

COLUMBIA 78s

STARDUST
ALL OF ME
NEW TIGER RAG, THE

IS NOT.

POLECAT
GORILLA
MOONGOOSE

GUINEA PIG

A CYCLE OF TELEPHONE
POLES
      EGGS—

  OSWALD
RUBBER
    HOW TO RIDE A HORSE

HOW TO PLAY
BASEBALL
VERSION B—

WILD ASS
     CHEETAH
MINK

64. Black Man, The

Statistic-
ian. Suspect.
Statue

Of limitations.
"That masked
Man." Alien-

able rights. Burden
Proof. Plea
Bargain. High

Blood pressures.
Triple
Double. Full court

Order. No contest.
Boom-
box not allowed

Train. Underground.
Off
Track, the record—spinning

A yarn. Bet. Rumor.
Research. Re-
hab.

Lab rat.
Art star.
Mascot—

Masochist, bad
Motha, mock
Turtle soup. Cock

roach. Oogabooga.
Congo-
lene. Buck

toothed lie gap.
RURAL LANDSCAPE
JUMBO MAGIC

BLACK SNAKES.
Macho. Castrado.
So-

phisticated.
"SPERMATAZOON."
Do not

Pass
Go directly to—
Assume

Position. PENIS
(SECTION). Spread
Eagled. Bruised

& blunt, burnt
By the mob
Till a doll—

Golliwog,
Sambo, breakfast
Butter.

Parkay! *Beurre
Noire.* Corporation
Of bones. IDEAL—

Face abstract
As Emmett Till
Drug

From the drink.
Evidence.
Suspend-

ed sentence.
[Expletive deleted]
Admit

One—emergency
Room—flat
Line. 10 cc IV. Stat.

65. Zydeco

three panels,
86 x 68 in. each

ICEBOX

She hex him
—you know—
done that hoo

doo—washed
his feet
iced down

WESTINGHOUSE©
his drink
buried his locks

his finger-
nails
like a coffin's

neath her front stoop

He's under a root
all smiles
His body stuffed,

doll to the devil—
FREEZER full
of pins, porcupine

pushover
He smells
of something

green, growing
He been
swamped

but good

EARLY SOUND FILM

SUBJECT
has been tense
lately, projecting—

complains of dreams
somnambulism—
convinced

he's being watched
boxed in
like a camera

Won't look
us in the eye
for fear

they are after him

When asked
about *they*
SUBJECT is vague

yet sure, scared
DON'T LOOK
IN THE CAMERA

Sees his father's
face everywhere
or says

he can stare
through skin
to men of bone, grins

Often he hears music

Treatment
does not seem
to be taking

We're afraid
SUBJECT
may pose

a threat to others
& himself
Recommend we

monitor situation carefully

SUBJECT him
to a battery
of tests, shock

treatment
his hair electric
a plucked banjo—

Fear
SUBJECT may
require

a museum
or some other form
of collective

corrective institution

In the mean
have prescribed
further medication

an art therapy regimen

PICK AX

Let the spiders
have their shoes
Let them live

& not rain

Let the beans stay
untranslated
black-eyed, jumping

Let sail
the suicides
Let the lepers in,

fingers fall

where they may
The piano go
to sea, tuneless

Let the ivories
return to tusk
WOOD

Let the spoons
quit washing
boards into song

Let the accordion
breathe
on its own

an iron lung

a singing scuba
Let speak
the MICROPHONE

the fiddle
be filled
with tokens for luck

Let the saints
march Let the ax
answer

66. Langston Hughes

LANGSTON HUGHES
LANGSTON HUGHES
     O come now
     & sang
them weary blues—

Been tired here
feelin low down
     Real
     tired here
since you quit town

Our ears no longer trumpets
Our mouths no more bells
     FAMOUS POET©—
     Busboy—Do tell
us of hell—

Mr Shakespeare in Harlem
Mr Theme for English B
     Preach on
     kind sir
of death, if it please—

We got not more promise
We only got ain't
     Let us in
     on how
you 'came a saint

LANGSTON
LANGSTON
     LANGSTON HUGHES
     Won't you send
all heaven's news

67. Logo

Out of the frying pan

& into the briars—
Brer Basquiat
with nickel bags

under his eyes.
Tar Baby. TRADE
MARK. The tracks

he lives across
own no sleep
car, no porter—

BUILT BY MEN
OF CHINA FOR CHUMP
CHANGE OF 1850—

Discovered, he done
left the underground
behind—passed by

his sticky *Black
Tar & Feathers,*
those barbed

wire halos
pointing heaven-
ward, askew.

THIS LAND USED TO BE
IN COTTON
USED TO BE IN VEGETABLES

NOW IT'S IN TOBACCO—

Tarpit-kept,
this indigo negro
charcoaled—

mammoth,
sabretooth—set
in a seal. IDEAL.

Hasbro. Behind him
ships steam. Rail
roaded. For Sale—

"Wild
Rabbits, Fresh
Coons." Cook till

brown & serve—

And there are people in these savage geographies
use your name in other contexts
think, perhaps, the title of your latest painting
another name for liar.

—AMIRI BARAKA (LEROI JONES)
"The Politics of Rich Painters"

They were people who went in for Negroes—Michael and
Anne—the Carraways. But not in the social-service, philan-
thropic sort of way, no. They saw no use in helping a race that was
already too charming and naive and lovely for words. Leave them
unspoiled and just enjoy them, Michael and Anne felt. So they
went in for the Art of Negroes—the dancing that had such jungle
life about it, the songs that were so simple and fervent, the poetry
that was so direct, so real. They never tried to influence that art,
they only bought it and raved over it, and copied it. For they were
artists, too.

—LANGSTON HUGHES
The Ways of White Folks

Went home and saw there was a party Mark Goodson was having
for Norman Lear, so I went over there, to One Beekman Place
(cab $4). Bianca was there with Carl Bernstein. Cindy and Joey
Adams were there and I brought up Roy Cohn and she said he
was on his last legs, that she'd seen him when he came into the
city for a small cocktail party someone gave for him. And a lady
was there and she said she's so bored since she stopped working
and her kids grew up and I said, "Why don't you adopt a Harlem
baby?" I told her how they're so cute and that if you go up there
and plunk your money down it's cash and carry.

—*The Andy Warhol Diaries*
THURSDAY, JUNE 19, 1986

DISC **2**: MOJO

Side **4** B-sides

68. NEW ART, NEW MONEY.
69. COLLABORATIONS. 1984.
70. HIS GLUE SNIFFING VALET.
71. IL PUBLICO BRUTO.
72. FOIS GRAS. 1984.
73. ANTAR.
74. NU-NILE. 1985.
75. WARHOL ATTENDS ROY COHN'S FINAL BIRTHDAY PARTY.
76. SURFACES: *a gallery of Warhol portraits*
77. PERUVIAN MAID OR, 3/4 OF OLYMPIA MINUS THE SERVANT.
78. VENUS.
79. LAST SUPPER. 1987.
80. SURFACES *(cont'd)*
81. GRAVESTONE. 1987.

82. MEMORIAL MASS FOR ANDY WARHOL. APRIL FOOL'S. 1987.
83. SHE INSTALLS CONFIDENCE & PICKS HIS BRAIN LIKE A SALAD.
84. SKETCHES OF A SHARK (STILL LIFE).
85. WARHOL ESTATE AUCTION. SOTHEBY'S 1988.
86. COLLECTION OF DENNIS HOPPER. 1987.

DISC **2**: MOJO

DISC TWO OF THE DOUBLE ALBUM

—SOME ASSEMBLY REQUIRED—

Side **4** B-sides

68. NEW ART, NEW MONEY.
69. COLLABORATIONS. 1984.
70. HIS GLUE SNIFFING VALET.
71. IL PUBLICO BRUTO.
72. FOIS GRAS. 1984.
73. ANTAR.
74. NU-NILE. 1985.
75. WARHOL ATTENDS ROY COHN'S FINAL BIRTHDAY PARTY.
76. SURFACES: *a gallery of Warhol portraits*
77. PERUVIAN MAID OR, 3/4 OF OLYMPIA MINUS THE SERVANT.
78. VENUS.
79. LAST SUPPER. 1987.
80. SURFACES *(cont'd)*
81. GRAVESTONE. 1987.

82. MEMORIAL MASS FOR ANDY WARHOL. APRIL FOOL'S. 1987.
83. SHE INSTALLS CONFIDENCE & PICKS HIS BRAIN LIKE A SALAD.
84. SKETCHES OF A SHARK (STILL LIFE).
85. WARHOL ESTATE AUCTION. SOTHEBY'S 1988.
86. COLLECTION OF DENNIS HOPPER. 1987.

DISC **2**: MOJO

{ Famous Boomerang }

I wanted to be a star, not a gallery mascot.
—JMB

68. New Art, New Money

New York Times Magazine
cover story, February 1985

Shoeless
like a '68 gold
medalist,

bronze. TIN.
ASBESTOS.
Fastest

in the world!
Poker-faced—
his brush raised

like cards, royal
flush, ace—
instead of black fist,

protest. Poster
boy wonder.
High roller—

his *Comme des Garçons*
uncivil suit
paint-splattered—

no U S A
across his chest,
no suede

pumas—
just the *bête noire*
beside him

a silhouette mute
on silver,
grinning. New art

new monkey
on his back—
black

balled. Kick
backs. Who's got
the short end

of this shtick?
Basquiat, Inc
in hock

trying to sell
passersby a painting
for two dollars—

FLAT FEE. Eliminate
the middle
man. Hoodoo

economics—needs
FILTER
CIGARETTES (TAXABLE).

TEN YEN. Give
to Fresh
Air Fund. Determined

as a Surgeon
General Warning:
smoking

like salmon,
he's swum up
the mainstream

to be caught
by camera—a fish
story out

of water, hooked.
Sinker. Loan
shark. Trickle down

etcetera—
his feet
bared & up

with his prices,
propped
on a chair toppled

like big game. The lion's
share. Free trade.
"Hob-nobs

with the hob-nobs"—
blue-chip Basquiat
playing the bull

market, stock-
broken. PESO NETO.
Sell-out

shows.
Whether garage,
rummage, lawn

or fire, such sales
can't last forever—
everything

must go. Black
Monday. Crashing
like a market,

going under—
Basquiat, Ltd
trades drugs

for arms,
swapping junk
bonds, futures.

B is anybody who helps me kill time.
B is anybody and I'm nobody. B and I.
I need B because I can't be alone. Except when I sleep.

Then I can't be with anybody.

—*The Philosophy of Andy Warhol*

69. Collaborations   { 1984 }

Warhol sets Basquiat
like a chain
smoke, or gang, to work

painting beside Warhol's brand,
his Arm
& Hammer. B kneeling

in white, abuzz, the two
doing an African master-
piece together. No sickle,

no Mao now—
B draws his seal encircling
another negro, this time

brown.
COMMEMORATIVE
crossed out, a coin

coming up heads.
ONE CENT. The black
bars across the frame

a censor's—
from our hero, the negro
's mouth, a horn

dangles like a pipe.
Let's call
a spade

a spade.
Could be Bird.
Could be

B blowing it
again, to coin
a phrase. Chump

change, two
bits—above the date
1955 in jailblock

letters: LIBERTY.

SOCIALITE

RUBBER RAT.
RUBBER
RAT. The head

209

of Spiderman
floating
EYE EYE

TEETH—
behind Your Friendly
Neighborhood

the headline
SOCIALITE
FIFTH AV

DEATH LEAP
hand-drawn
by Warhol, slinger

of webs—*Where are you*
going to Spiderman
Nobody knows

who you are—
social butterfly
—LEECHES—scaling high

rises, Empire.

ALBA'S BREAKFAST

ABC's—Andy
Warhol, Basquiat
& Francesco Clemente

surround a table, empty
bowls, day's supply
of vitamin D.

Paint on plates
TOAST EGGS
BACON COFFEE

"   FAST SPECIAL"
"M*GR PLEASE."
B's close-cropped

hair, elegant
in well-starched
shirt, black jacket

like flak. Bullet
proof, bus
boy—Short

Order Cannibal
Wanted.
Draws a head

beside Clemente's
mouth open
his wife ALBA©

ALBA. For his own
face, Warhol places
—"L*T M* GO"—

a machine, washing.

NEGRESS

Black bars
—a supermarket
code across her chest

—R.SGS TMK—
hair flipped
like a 60s girl-group

Felix the Cat
grinning, going
wild—

How-To
for a bow-tie.
Some of my

best blacks
are my friends.
STEEP INCLINE

GIN—B
& W standing
beside the painting

not smiling. ZENITH.
1/2 1/2 1/2—
good help is hard

to bind—your waiter
for today—silhouette,
servant—*Gin-Soaked*

Critics panning
like fool's gold
—SHOT GLASS—the show.

EVERLAST

Mismatch—FIXED

FIGHT—black
turtlenecked
Warhol in shorts, white

wig. ROBE. GLOVES.
GLASS
JAW. Bare-chested

Basquiat, fists
cross his chest
as if at a wake,

his own. LADIES
+ GENKS. WHITE
TRUNKS. In this

coroner—the challenger—
his hair
electric, posed

with W's mitt
mashed against his face
facing-off. RABBIT

PUNCH. Combination,
jab, upper
hand—EVERLAST

on both belts, going
toe-to-toe. After
making the rounds—

Shafrazi + Bischofberger
present—promote—
the critics weigh in

B OOOOO
& the show don't sell.
B retreats, splits

—decision—
won't take no seconds
SMARTENING UP A CHUMP

no lip.

"The black person is the protagonist in most of my paintings," he says. "I realized that I didn't see many paintings with black people in them." Some of the figures are taken from life. For example, one powerful painting was drawn from a sad old man in a wheelchair whom Basquiat saw on a neighborhood street last spring. "He would say to the young Puerto Rican helping him, 'Put me in the sun, put me in the sun.' He was a Cajun, from Louisiana. I gave him some money and he wanted to hug me, to pull me in. I pulled back." But the vision is transformed in Basquiat's bold painting. It is saturated with red, the wheelchair like a throne, the old man almost a god whose head is a primitive mask, frightening and defiant.

—CATHLEEN MCGUIGAN
"New Art, New Money"

70. His Glue-Sniffing Valet

Prodigy, prodigal
son—he's sick
of being called

Warhol's protegé,
lap dog. Mascot.
Lawn

jockey. Negro
for Hire—avail.
for promos, parties

public
& private. Inside
like a joke

a job, he tires
of his titles—
bad boy, cash

cow, emblem.
SCALO MERCI
on an elephant's

trunk, tusks
blunted—he just cain't
seem to forget.

Trouble the water.

The Cajun—
visitation, visage—
bares his teeth

from a wheelchair,
his valiant friend
behind him

bellowing for change,
begging. Shoulders
OATS like a wt. *Wade*

in the water, children—

Withdrawal.
B recoils, draws
back, then paints

the pair all night—
His Glue-Sniffing
Valet. Lackey.

Understudy.
Bridesmaid. Media
darling—*It's all over*

but the crying.

Takes the *Come*
painting, glue
gooey, that Andy gave him

—a rare bird—
& gave it away
or burnt it

but good. *Bridge*
o'er trouble water.
O to be young

gifted & black
balled! enfant
terrible—smackhead—

an equal opportunist
destroyer. Harmful
if swallowed. Brat,

bat boy, idiot
savant. Read
the fine print—Not

responsible
for loss damage
delay or Acts

of God. *God*
don't like ugly—
And He ain't stuck

on pretty. Boy
Friday. Sunday
painter, Tuesday child,

Yesterday's news.
Rock cried out—
no hiding place.

Johnny come
lately (if
ever). Jack

of all trade.
What's-
his-face.

71. Il Publico Bruto

How they come round
at all hours
not even a knock

A. WHOLESELLERS
B. RETAILERS
C. BULLSHITTERS

Circle like a pack
of hyenas
or Lucky Strikes, or sharks

w/ six sets of teeth—

O. SHINBONE (TIBIA)
P. NIPPLES
Q. NAVEL

Blood going back
into an arm
asleep, that prickle

pain—a sucker-
fish borne
every minute, a cicada

saying *seventeen*
—THE FOOT—his days
numbers

1. FOR THE IMPORTATION OF
2. FOR SUPPLYING LONDON WITH
   CAPTIAL, THREE MILLIONS

3. FOR BUILDING AND REBUILDING
4. FOR MAKING OF MUSLIN
5. FOR CARRYING ON AND IMP

He cain't
get a show to save
his life

PABLO BEGINS
TO DRAW & PAINT
ATTENDS BULLFIGHT

WITH FATHER
"PICADOR"
FIRST PAINTING

Taxmen, toreadors
contentenders—
what cd've been

JOE LOUIS BILLY CONN
JACK DEMPSEY GENE TUNNEY
ROCKY MARCIANO JERSEY JOE

JOE FRAIZER
Some wiseguy at party:
Q: What do you do

A: "Manage a McDonalds"
AUTO-NO-FAN
And the man walks away

Some say to his face
he painted better
on junk

FIRST COMMUNION
BREEDING HORSES
BOWL OF CREAM

Bull-
fighter, valkyrie,
auctioneer—

PABLO BEGINS TO
DRAW AND ATTENDS
AND PAINT

HIS EARLIEST PICTURE

If the bull
stays standing
no one throws

roses, thorns
¡Olé!
Instead he's set free

There were articles in the papers about the police arresting the "Sidney Poitier and Diahann Carroll son" for being an imposter. He was staying at all these people's houses. Halston was smart that time, right away he told him to leave. You could just tell in a second that this kid was lying. But these other people all let him stay at their houses! I mean, he could have been anybody, he could have just wiped out a whole family.

—*The Andy Warhol Diaries*
WEDNESDAY, OCTOBER 19, 1983

72. Fois Gras   { 1984 }

Well-heeled
& bred, manored,
what got him

into the houses
was not what
he plead

but how—he spoke
such conviction
we could hardly deny

or believe. Here
he was—fabulous,
speaking five tongues

& polite, nothing
like the news—
no gun, no sob

story, he was son
of the *Raisin*
in Sun star—

The Defiant One—
what's his name
again—Poitier,

Sidney, *Who Came to Din-*
Din, a doctor. *Sir.* You know those West
Indians just work harder.

PIONEERS EMIGRANTS
METAL ALLOY—
No urchin, the boy knew

our daughters (but not
too well); our sons
he spoke of

highly. Parlayed
their nick
names, the best year

for wine—he was sweet.
Who knew how off
he was—in the arts

we thought, not
touched. SAND
PAINTING RITUAL

FOR A SICK CHILD
NAVAHO—
his mother was Diahann Carroll

after all. A delight.
He was a vacation, a light-
soaked place. PATE

DE FOIS GRAS. He spoke
on things like they
were real, never dull

— VENUS
— PYRAMIDS OF MYCERNIUS
— PABLO PICASSO BULL'S

    HEAD 1941—
    HANDLE BARS +
    BYCICLE SEAT.

What a ride
we were on!
For the life

of us, who knew
how many knocks
"SUN WORSHIPING"

he'd took, or made
across the city?
We first greeted

him so dubious
WHITE KID GLOVES
that his sober Hullo

seemed sane. Safe.
BONJOUR EFFECT
(ED). Understood

how, stranded, he needed
us—this much
to which we were used.

Accustomed. Giving
was one thing
—wounded bison

—our inner
city charities—but living
with, another. Here he was

larger than life—at least
ours—& we loved it!
Who knows how

many homes he'd hit—
AFTER JENKINS
MRS W.M.

MRS S. MRS GW—
That boy deserved
an Oscar, not his father—

1. RAHOTEP IS SHOWN DARKER
   THAN HIS WIFE
2. CREAM PITCHER

3. TOOTHPICK HOLDER.
   The first one—
   excepting

help—not whom
we knew, but who knew
where we lived. How.

He barely took
a thing—just food
& trust. Such taste!

No one taught
him that.
(On him handcuffs

never did fit.)
Imposer
imposter—PLACID

GLASS EYE—he was pretty.
Beautiful, like a mulatto
girl. Lispy.

Made such
an impression, fuss—
doppleganger, dead

ringer, cause
celebre. Taken
in, we were fools

full of ourselves—
BEAUTIFUL
FALSE TEETH—fell

for that charm,
his tom-
foolery.

73. Antar

Mouthful
of stars, cold
sores, tooth

not yet gone—
his gapped grin
like Rousseau's

Sleeping Gypsy—
the rainbow
hair & cloak

at which Lion sniffs
curious
patient. Hungry.

Gravy. Will he
wake? We want
him to & don't

want to know
what might devour
him—King

of Jungle, Lord
Beast.
Signifying

Monkey throwing
down doo
doo. Blue

night. Talking
shit—Hey Lion,
Elephant say he cd kick

your ass like a bad
habit—jive-end-
jive—say you're a chump

or dead. Or both.
All them
lies. Makes you see

stars, wish some cold
could rain & lick
these bones away—

74. Nu-Nile   { 1985 }

He's known rivers.

Seen the waves
a fragrant
pomade

laid deep in his hair—
sat down
beneath the barber's chair

& felt the cream
whiten his cheeks,
a straight-edge razor

slapped against leather
cutting his face
like a stash. Gauge.

Roach. SPOONS
SHARPENED TO CUT
FLOUR WITH WHITE

LEAD. He's read
enough to know
the steady undertow

of spleen, drawing
him down—
felt the pain of poison

the flash flood
following heavy veins.
He's no river—

yet rushed
three days to finish
the Palladium's

Mike Todd Room,
a mural wide
as Mississippi

—NOTARY©—
seen the crowns
of the Congo, drums

like tins of hair grease
fighting crocodile curls,

a conk's tears.
He's laid down, spent,
beside the Lethe

& seen the sunset
come & sunrise & still
his eyes open, riveted—

thought himself dead
till he heard his own
blood's ebb. His skin sold

—grown thin—downriver.

The night the Palladium opened, it felt like you were in Saigon during the last days with the helicopters coming down and everyone hysterical to get on. People were diving under the ropes, it was so dramatic. When I was going in, everyone dived underneath me and the bouncers ran over to help Haoui and Sally—the doormen—and in my mind it seems like the bouncers had machine guns. Of course they didn't, but it was like that kind of feeling. Suddenly I was pushed back into the club and they pulled down those heavy metal gates like garage doors—and people were diving under them as they came down, rolling around on the concrete floor in their tuxedos and evening gowns, desperate to get in.

—MADELAINE NETTER
Andy Warhol's Party Book

75. Warhol Attends Roy Cohn's Final Birthday Party at the Palladium, June 1985

Welcome, won't you sit
down sir, the whole
world's here. Who's she

with? What's he think
he's wearing? Warhol dishes
the guest list, giving

friends dirt the next day.
Cohn in the crowd, center,
feeble but no one

asks. From the walls
monitors lower
the boom—Cohn

back in the day, cheeks
full. Bald. Bow-tied.
Dozen-faced. Speaks

about Red Tide, those pinkos
in the Cabinet. Closet
cases. Names his black

list, where we're all
guests. Domino effect—
Warhol thinks back to the Love

Boat where he played
himself—was the nine hundred
ninety-ninth guest—

his snapshot beside Isaac
the black bar-
tender, the mermaids, the party

where they paraded
past guests cursed to appear
in the life preserver

who'd since died —Ethel Merman,
Peter Lawford, Slim Pickens—
then the lucky thousandth

guest announced! Where is
Warhol's name on the roll?
Balloons fall like dirigibles

the cake battleship-big
covered in Old Glory. Singing.
Candles blown out

with some help Cohn rises
to talk, thanks, the years
have been good—

from the rafters God
Bless America & the shredded
plastic flag unfurls—

Cohn soon dead, secreted
like the dark hair, buried
awkward, beneath Warhol's wig.

76. Surfaces

a gallery of Warhol portraits

I paint pictures of myself to...I guess, yeah, to remind myself that I'm still around.
—ANDY WARHOL

**SELF-PORTRAIT
BY ANDY WARHOL   1986**

Camouflage-filled,
his face
looms red

& pink & white,
splotched like
his skin. Looks

out at us—hair
storebought,
standing on end—

at attention—shocked.
What took him
till now to return

hidden, army
enemy, enigma?

**INSIDE THE FORBIDDEN CITY, BEIJING,
PHOTOGRAPHED BY CHRISTOPHER MAKOS   1982**

Enigmas, enemies—
Warhol can't tell Chinese
faces apart. Envies

their anonymity, the same
army hats, little red books,
dark hair. Silver-maned

Warhol pursued
by a film crew. Who's this
clown, powdered,

mimicking the giant stone
lions—*great footage*—buying
junk by the luggageful? Gone

229

north, climbing the Great Wall
breathless—*grimace*—well spent.

ANDY WARHOL DRAWN
BY JEAN-MICHEL BASQUIAT   1984

Grimacing, or well, or mouthless—
Basquiat does not
know how best

to draw Andy
out—flat, flush
right—

unarmed Warhol
like a PEZ
dispenser, unful-

filled. Underfed.
Sickly Andy opens
up—talking

out both sides
of his neck.

BROWN SPOTS

Drella, big
wig, head
banana—rolling

in bread. Shopaholic.
Bruises easy. Skin peeled
back reveals

pale flesh. Jaundice.
Collagen injections. Works
out with Basquiat, wishes

he could tan. *Yes,
we have no* cure for such dis-
color—going bananas

& through trash, a millionaire
saving batteries for copper.

BASQUIAT PAINTED
BY ANDY WARHOL IN THE MANNER
OF MICHELANGELO'S DAVID 1984

Saved. Copper-
colored—not
the pale marble

of the original—
nor Warhol's black
version with B all

dissected, kaleidoscopic
as gossip. Here he's not
even naked. Jock

strap. Hand half-raised
like a student's. SLINGSHOT.
Warhole's subject red

as a target, butt of
jokes. The king's clothes.

WARHOL AT THE HOTEL PRINCIPE
DI SAVOIA IN MILAN, PHOTOGRAPH BY
CHRISTOPHER MAKOS 1987

Open-mouthed, hands
cross his crotch—
Warhol reclines, legs thin

in long johns,
socks. Glasses on.
Something FOOTBALL

across his chest
like an S. Eyes shut.
One month—less—

from death, his face
pain-defined, contort-
ed. Defies. Drawn

like breath. Wigged.
White.

I confront the problem of how to look at a maid only when I'm staying at a European hotel or when I'm a guest at somebody else's house. It's so awkward when you come face to face with a maid. I've never been able to pull it off. Some people I know are very comfortable looking at maids and even telling them what they'd like done, but I can't handle it. When I go to a hotel, I find myself trying to stay there all day so the maid can't come in. I make a point of it. Because I just don't know where to put my eyes, where to look, what to be doing while they're cleaning. It's actually a lot of work, avoiding the maid, when I think about it.

—*The Philosophy of Andy Warhol*

77. Peruvian Maid
   or, 3/4 of Olympia
   Minus the Servant

      While in Europe
we heard this story, which
like all stories, is true:
a maid was hired in a hurry
to replace the well-loved, long-term,
live-in housekeeper
at the house we were staying in
for free—she'd cook
& clean & generally keep
up the place.
           A friend
of the family's, a kid
really, was having trouble:
his father drinking them
both dry. ABSINTH. Out of house
& home. Even money has its limits,
like men.
           One day, between drunks,
the father begged his son to save
them both, to go under
Lake Geneva & take
from their vault all he could
& sell it.
           The son did—
like anyone else would—found
row after row of paintings,
Mapplethorpes, even
that famous one of Warhol
pale, successful, eyes
closed, almost dead.
           We saw that
one ourselves, casually leaned
against the wall like a broom.
           Gathered
the father had been quite
a collector in the 80's
art boom bull
market & didn't even know
what he had.
           After counting
& cataloguing & asking
artwise friends what
the work was worth, the son sold
many pieces, mostly for cash. He kept
some *objets* at his friend's family
home—along with thousands
in Swiss francs—in order
not to tempt his father's
swimming will.

One morning
while the son lounged,
sunning beside the family
friend's pool, the new maid
came out to ask—*en français*
no doubt—whether
he wanted anything
cool to drink.
    He did,
merci. She went inside again
only to rush
out to the driveway—he would
have said 'carport'—duck into
her subcompact, then zoom
backwards out the long, pebbly,
private drive. A little fast
for groceries, no? For
lemonade?
    Then it struck him—
rushed upstairs to check
his briefcase—gone
was the cash, every penny
—or is it *centime* —each
colored bill.
    The maid may not
have been Peruvian, but North
African or Senegalese,
less likely the shade
of Olympia's servant
than the color of Olympia
herself.
    They found her
car at the French border,
figured, back home, she could live
on the money for seven
years, ten. Well.
    What
would you have done? The money
there, mottled, still greener
than any future you had
imagined—despite creature
comforts of work, a roof.
    Back home
the family you hadn't seen
for years, father not growing
any younger, mother becoming
more bent.
    We each pay
in different ways: FROM THE VAPOR
OF GASOLINE Basquiat's maid said,
charcoal scrawl on slats of white wood.

78. Venus

Now Venus you know
was loaded with charms
and look at what happened to her

Waiting around
She's minus two arms
Could happen to me? No sir.

—*An Imitation of Life* (1959)
Douglas Sirk, dir.

ABUELITA

We's all start
out that way
We don't get dumb

till later. Aunt
Delilah's
Pancake Shop

32 Million Sold.
I just gave out
all of a sudden—

Tain't nothin.
Things
is workin. Leave

him be.
Leave him be.
She am

an angel Miss B—
O Don't say
Mammy—

Louise Beavers big
as a tree, puts on,
shines, her chain-

saw smile—

BIG JOY

Paroxysms!
Paradise!
Post-prandial

bliss! She's
got her head on
tight, wrapped

in gauze—a mummy—
mammy—
hanky head.

Her words behind her
collusion
collage

Rorsharch test.
And what do we see
today? Mother::

Father. Dog::
Father.
The Farmer picks

his wife wife
picks the child
hi ho

the merry o—
it's time for our
meds. Pills bright hidden

beneath her tongue, held.

DOG BITE

The white girl playing

the black girl
who looks
white keeps running

away, shows off
them legs long
letting the seams

on her stockings gleam.
Even her dark Mama
calls her Miss

Linda now—pretend
she don't know
her, her own

flesh. "I'm somebody
else. I'm white
white! white!"—

passing while
her mother passes
away—LEFT

like a hand. Hears
& needs only
the applause

at H'woods
Moulin Rouge—not
her mother's plea—

No more weeping
& wailing (x 2)
sings Mahalia

at the funeral
Mama put away
plenty money for—

No more trouble
in this world
No more Dorothy

Dandridge drowned
in dope—dancing—
on fire

~~HOLLYWOOD AFRICANS~~
~~PART TWO~~
No Butterfly

McQueen
in her one room throne
cocooned, broke, old & cold

going up
after lighting, to keep
warm, the kerosene—

MAD

From bighouse
to bughouse—
the looney

bin, booby
hatch—doctors
dull her down

with drugs.
What,
me worry?

Sheepish, she's funny
farmed out. *Spy*
vs Spy, white

shooting up black.
Flying. Next stop—
Insomnia Valley

1. "VOYAGE TO THE BOTTOM SEA"
2. ALFRED E. NEUMAN
3. ALFRED HITCOCK (HIS FACE OVER

& OVER). Do not unbuckle
or stand until
we come to a complete

halt. First
put the mask
—breathe regular—

over nose mouth—
then assist any small child
you might be traveling

with. Please keep
in mind
the best exit

may be behind you—

79. Last Supper   { 1987 }

It went
well, as expected,
& here you are

Mr Warhol, awake
with your fear
of hospitals, gall

bladder gone—
though Bob Robert (not his real
name) signed in

it was Andy
who went under, out,
Andy whose insides

—gangrenous, snaking—
got opened up
again. Sewn. New

scar to match
his missing
spleen, half

a lung—the shooting
pain, now ancient, still
shown on his skin.

Andy did you
think of death
or did it think

of you? The woman
under long dark
hair, seemed to follow

him across Europe—
She's trying to do
me in! It took time

a lot of talking
to calm
your nerves. Flew

back two days early
for the operation
& here Warhol is, his

extra parts missing
like his clothes—no bladder
or tape recorder,

just the television
overhead
like God. Talking.

The private nurse is nice.
No thanks,
I'll eat later—

Warhol in the place
he dreads,
that h-word

he can't even say
much less
be driven past, avoided

since he was shot.
TRUSS CORSET
TRACTION. He's read

every thing he was
brought
or tried—*Dreamgirl*

& the gossip
columns, *His Way*.
BE A SOMEBODY

WITH A BODY. Eat
something. Shoot
you up to stop

the pain—Warhol
sitting up
on a quiet ward.

The walls sky.
Future open as his side,
healing. Am I

the most famous
person admitted?
Should I

do more *Last
Suppers?* All Italy
seemed to love them—

storming in
when, across the street,
DaVinci's lines

were too long. Thousands
crossed the Corso
Magenta to see

the refectory full
of your latest
silk screens—

bikes revving
behind the Big C
like Hell's

Angels, price
placed over
Christ's head—

6⁹⁹. *Dove*
soap. Bread. Monocled
Mr Peanut,

a lung in a top-hat
tapdancing—
GE—we bring

good things
to life.
Where's that nurse?

It's late. repent
AND SIN NO MORE.
Warhol needs

ARE YOU "DIFFERENT"?
something like attention.
HEAVEN

& HELL ARE JUST
ONE BREATH AWAY!
No prayer or Hail

Mary can help—
THE ONLY WAY
OUT IS IN.

The nurse from Avalon
asleep or deep
in her Bible—Paul,

Romans, Revelations—
Warhol alone on
this white wing,

growing stiff as a brand
new bill—fifty,
a hundred, a face

fading green.

80. Surfaces

cont'd

AUTOPSY

Side of his neck—
the thick perfume
of end—chest

cut into wings, angeled
Warhol opened
up—for once. *Eau*

de toilette. Still
with his wig on—
cause of death

unknown. Atomizer. What
weather he's under
like a knife—yesterday

sitting up, full recovery—today
cold, embalmy, mostly cloudy.

WARHOL TIME CAPSULE   1980s

Guns, Knives, Myths.
Goethes, Stadiums.
The Brooklyn Bridge.

Details of Renaissance
Paintings, Munchs,
Endangered

Species. Ads.
Campbell Soup
Boxes, Cars, Flowers,

Frederick the Greats,
Self-Portraits.
Beethovens. Cowboys

& Indians. Unfinished History
of American TV.

ANDY WARHOL ON TELEVISION
IN MIAMI BEACH, FLORIDA,
PHOTOGRAPHED BY CHRIS MAKOS   1987

It was TV told the photographer
his friend had gone—
not the clerk who handed

him his key & mentioned Andy
was over—TV that turned
on, cleared its throat

& confirmed Warhol's name,
fame, that same god-
damn quote. More

like 15 seconds, baby—
just enough to get off
a few shots. Stills—saves

the last time, grainy, any
would see Andy.

WARHOL MODELS WITH MILES
DAVIS AT TUNNEL   1987

See Andy live
with Miles, See Andy parade
the runway for Ford

Modeling Agency, taxiing
like an airplane. Bored
into by pain just days

before he dies, Warhol paces
backstage, about
to burst. VERVE. *Bye Bye*

Blackbird. Trails
the catwalk for the finale,
carrying Miles' long tails—

alligator fur lace—the pain
showing, at last, on his face.

JEAN-MICHEL BASQUIAT EATING,
PHOTOGRAPHED BY ANDY WARHOL

Warhol's last show (almost)
like a breath—Basquiat
's mouth open, about

to fork in food
like a road—
nine shots of him sewn

together as if surgery,
Andy's serrated side, cut
too many times to count.

Now even Warhol's gall wants out.
Though there in black & white
for B it's difficult

to swallow, stomach, make sense
how quick (like that!) he went.

I never understood why when you died, you didn't just vanish, and everything could just keep going the way it was only you just wouldn't be there. I always thought that I'd like my own tombstone to be blank. No epitaph, and no name. Well actually, I'd like it to say "Figment."

—ANDY WARHOL

81. Gravestone   { 1987 }

Breaking ground.
Root
work. Dirt

nap. Trip-
tych—three doors
unhinged. Pearly

gates. Our boy's
done lost it—
Warhol's gone.

For good. Staring
walls, skulls—
Basquiat paints

Andy's elegy—
~~PERISHABLE.~~
PERISH-

ABLE. Post-
mortemism.
Factotum

pole. Green
thumb. Grounds
keeper. Boo

hoo doo—
floor crawling
with art, Uncle

Andy's Ant Farm.
DT's. Bottled up
djinnis. Cartoons.

Finger food.
B bawling, crash
& burn. Rose.

Ghost story.
Skeleton
key. Anno

Domini.

Going to funerals is a good way to remember who's dead. I try to avoid funerals, but if you don't go to them it's easy to forget who's in heaven—acquaintances die and three months later I'm back to asking people how they are.

—*Andy Warhol's Party Book*

82. Memorial Mass for Andy Warhol, April Fool's Day, 1987

Some say he's a saint
Others he's not
dead yet

That that robot
from Japan
made a perfect match

Or a facsimile
laid in state
That he's changed

his name
& moved Upstate
Whatever they say

one thing's set—
Andy's out
of it, his phone's cut

he can't be reached
Some say
he's a ghost

That he's only gone
to Bloomingdale's
shopping

Think what you want

Andy's not
here, didn't get
an invite

& is more
than upset
His former assistant

Gerard Malanga
wears the front-
page of the *Post*—

ANDY WARHOL DEAD
AT 58
silk-screened on a T-shirt

Andy's kaput
& loves
this fuss, the mass

of people, the host
every last
minute

Front row, Basquiat's
sorrow-shot,
all salt

The lunch at the Diamond Horseshoe following the memorial mass was the most atypical "Andy Warhol party" anyone had ever been to—no crashers, and no Andy. All the different phases and facets of his life came together, from his relatives up from Pittsburgh to Timothy Leary and Viva, from Don Johnson to Philip Johnson to Jed Johnson, from Dominique de Menil to Raquel Welch. People looked around and realized the impact Andy had had on their lives: Who could Lou Reed and Ann Bass ever had in common except Andy? Where else could Claus Von Bülow hug Debbie Harry?

—Andy Warhol's Party Book

83. She Installs Confidence
& Picks His Brain Like a Salad

A hard
hoe to row—
act to follow

vamp vixen
venus (genus:
girlfriend). *Self-Portrait*

with Suzanne.
Big Shoes.
Playing

the numbers
the nigger pool
he's hit

3 day straight.
Please quit
calling

we have a winner—

it's all Goode
(Jennifer that is)
in this lottery

drawing lots
the last straw.
The camel's back

in bidness—
gotten over
the hump by

a hair. How's this
for a start—
head over to Area

& the Invisible
Sculpture
where once Warhol stood

then left
blank & sold
the space—STERILE

DESTROY
AFTER SINGLE
USE. The club

changes like a bridge
group, month
to month. Trumped.

He's smitten. He's done
pretending like the Living
Unicorn, that goat

with a horn grafted
into his head—fêted
at the Palladium

for being a freak.
The first. One night
only! Here at Area

the sharks pace
their tank, mouths
open & closing like a bouquet

of flesh-
eating flowers—
centerpiece. Venus

flytrap. Cakewalk. Goode
w/ her bad self
& he stepping

out, into the light—

84. Sketches of a Shark (Still Life)

Tiger, Sand, Great White

nearsighted, can smell
1 oz. of blood
in million parts water

no air
bladder, must
keep moving

or die of anoxia

Dogfish, Hammerhead

may never sleep
some found hundred feet
deep, floating, dozing

in underwater caves
apparently able to store
food or foreign objects

in stomach for weeks—
plankton & other fish
a television

a bulldog
(head & forelegs)
the leash still attached

Dusky, Whitetip, Lemon

one taken in the Adriatic Sea
contained 3 overcoats
(not their wearers)

a raincoat, license plate
parts of horse
a ham—

suggest shark, not whale
where Jonah lived
3 days

Makos, Grey Nurse, Land

sandpaper skin
distinct
dorsal, no gills

as many as twenty-five
thousand teeth
in 10 years

sharp jagged sawlike
replaced in rows
like tombstones

Zambeszi, Lake Nicaragua, Ganges

a taste for corpses
burned & buried
by the riverside

The Navy-Smithsonian
Shark Attack File—
deep or shallow

water, all
temperatures
once believed blind

like a bull, when attacking

Porbeagle, Angel

beautiful,
myopic, mis-
understood creatures

we know now
how they strike
from below

85. Warhol Estate Auction, Sotheby's, 1988

The crowds coil
around the side
    of the bldg, wanting

    to snake inside & see
what Warhol left—
        emerald jewelry, Salvador Dali

    ear clips, Keith Haring
Swatches still
        in their boxes—he opened

    little toward what
few knew was the end,
        buying & throwing

    bags in ornate rooms
until even the help couldn't
        shoulder them open. Crowd winds

    like a watch, a yo-
yo, a cobra
        hypnotized—

    you are getting sleepy—
waiting for the cookie
        jars to come up—Lot

    no.   , in groups
of three. Empty.
        The bids begin high

    in the hundreds
& soon soar far past
        possible—sets he bought

    for a ten-spot go now
for $1980—11 thousand
        dollars for a Natn'l Silver

    Mammy. Warhol's on
a roll, would love to have
        been here, but nothing

is cheap & he would hate to see
the junk he fought for,
        found, go

away like he did—prone
like Jasper Johns' *Light*
        Bulb drawn

or bronzed, asleep
on its platform.
        Cast your bid

for a bit of him, history—the Deco
chairs & desks, the *Mirror*
        by Lichtenstein, his *Smiling*

Cat—to own the Fiesta
ware his shelves
        once sagged with, unable

to be eaten
off of. Could it be these bright
        bowls that killed him, paint

poisoning his stomach?
The Rolls Royce, the Man
        Ray & Norman Rockwells,

his Cy Twomby which went
just shy of a million.
        Let the bidding

begin—fifteen
from the gentleman
        in the back? Going

once, twice—
Section 14—
        this 19th c. Negro

Boxer on the block,
a pugilist with arms
        of wood, always raised

—Sold.

86. Collection of Dennis Hopper   { 1987 }

HEART AS ARENA—
Hopper in a docu-trauma
discussing Warhol

after his own comeback,
seated before
his giant Basquiat—

PROMETHEUS.
BLACK TEETH.
Andy's already bit

the dust
& Basquiat's just
about to—DEBT (SIC)

PISS PASSPORT
FREE KIT LIGHT RED
PAYING DUES.

Since Hopper's
debut he's lived
hard & died

none—seen
the best stars
of his degeneration

deep in reef-
er madness.
RELIGIOUS

TALK GETS FREE
MEAL. EROICA.
THE OBSERVATORY

FROM THE JAMES
DEAN MOVIE—
behind him

a beaten brown
head blurts out
VICIOUS DOG EAR WAX

POURING POWDERED ROCK
OR EARTH OF VARIOUS
COLORS AND PAINTING

FOR A SICK CHILD.
Hopper's hairline
has made only a brief

retreat—widow's
peak—much the same
ATOMIZED

SHRINE SKULL
as when Warhol
painted him in a ten-gallon

hat, whisky smile
as in his *Last Movie*
which wasn't. ALCOHOL

IN THIS TOWN
SENATE INVESTIGATION
CHAMPION SHIP BOUT—

wears that same squint
seen in *Giant*
or *Rebel without*

a Cause—
JAWBONE
OF AN ASS

BIRD
OF PARADISE—
Jimmy Dean rolling

out the cliff-bound
car, T-Bird or Mercury,
just before it soars—

Side **5** Solos

87. CHARLIE CHAN ON HORN.
88. SAVOY.
89. RIDDLE ME THIS BATMAN.
90. NATURE MORTE. 1988.
91. LIGHT BLUE MOVERS. 1987.
92. PIG LATIN.
93. PORTRAIT OF THE ARTIST AS A YOUNG DERELICT.
94. OREO. 1988.
95. CALCIUM. 1988.
96. VICTOR 25448. 1987.
97. THE MECHANICS THAT ALWAYS HAVE A GEAR LEFT OVER.
98. TO BE TITLED.
99. PEGASUS. 1988.
100. RIDING WITH DEATH. 1988.

101. WILL & TESTAMENT.
102. KALIK. 1988.
103. EROICA. 1988.
104. TV STAR. 1988.
105. HAIKU.
106. THE PICTURES: *second run*
107. TWO PHOTOGRAPHS OF JEAN-MICHEL BASQUIAT. PARIS.
108. PENTIMENTO.
109. SOUL.
110. THE NINTH CIRCLE.
111. EPITAPH.
112. SHRINE OUTSIDE BASQUIAT'S STUDIO. SEPTEMBER 1988.
113. VANITAS.
114. RELICS.
115. HEAVEN. 1985.
116. URGENT TELEGRAM TO JEAN-MICHEL BASQUIAT.
117. RETROSPECTIVE.

DISC **2**: MOJO

{ Out Getting Ribs }

Subjective halos may be considered as the result of a conflict between the light and a living surface. From the conflict between the exciting principle and the excited, an undulating motion arises, which may be illustrated by a comparison with the circles on water. The stone thrown in drives the water in all directions; the effect attains a maximum, it reacts, and being opposed, continues under the surface. The effect goes on, culminates again, and thus the circles are repeated.

—JOHAN WOLFGANG VON GOETHE
Theory of Colours

87. Charlie Chan On Horn

For Prestige

Bird records
a few sides
(for contract

reasons) as Mr Charlie
Chan—no matter
the name his blues

sound the same,
same alto blaring
ALCHEMY,

licks exotic
as *Charlie Chan
in Black Magic*—

Chan's dark sidekick
Birmingham Brown
(a.k.a. Man-

tan Moreland)
seeing ghosts,
fleeing. *Feets*

do yo stuff—
THRIVING ON A RIFF,
Bird on a run

(in one place)
eyes bugged out
blowing

like Gabriel.
Solos snorted—
in one nose

& out the other.
Gone. Number one
son—don't they know

Charlie Chan
is a white man?
Fu Manchu too.

(Bless you.)
Parker play
your horn, not

no coon
no coolie in a white
suit. Bird's shot

his way to the top—
made a fist, tied off
& caught

the first vein
out of town.
Laying tracks—

NOWS THE TIME
NOWS THE TIME
BIRD GETS THE WORM—

Now dig
this—Basquiat
lit, lidded, does

a gravestone—
CPRKR
in the Stan-

hope Hotel,
the one Bird bit
the dust in (ON AIR)

high. TEETH.
HALOES
FIFTY NINE CENT.

Who knew how well
Basquiat would follow—
feet (six deep) first.

88. Savoy

To tango
To solo
To Jump

Jim Crow
To wallflower
To twist again

like we did
WATERCOOLED
last summer

To dance card
& contest
To shake

it to the east
the west
To split

To ain't got
that swing
To two-

step
To swig
SHINING SHOES

IN ST. LOUIS
SHINING SHOES
IN ST. LOUIS

To can-can
ENGINE, GAS
To last

request
To toot-toot
tootsie

goodbye
To dip
RIBBON RELEASE

To tap
HEY! HEY!
HYENA

BABOON
To Eagle Rock
To turkey

trot
"Snakehips"
To horse

around
ASCENT
To regret

To forage
& forget
COLLECT

ALL 12
To nickel
& dime to death

FLIES FLIES
FLIES FLIES FLIES
FLIES FLEAS

To jive
To jig
To rent

party & flop
wally
To shim-sham

shimmy
To shag
To speakeasy

Get off that dime!
To cut
a rug, slow

drag, Charleston
Lindy Hop
To cakewalk

DECOMPISITON
OF WATER
"JOHN

THE REVELATOR"

To God
& part
way back

89. Riddle Me This Batman

Doesn't everyone die
a dozen
times, ready

or not? ZLONK!
KAPOW! @;#$%*!?!
The cancer

slow, or sudden
as heart's failure—
desire desire—whether

suicide or mass
murder, we all
share final

breath. Rites.
Residuals.
To the Batetcetera

Robin! driving
crazy, the panicked
power pole he wraps

his car around—
is ours,
that last prayer, even

if only a shopping
list, some milky
thing. *Must*—

reach—
utility—
belt—too many

spinoffs in the works
too many arch-
villains going

makes things easy for.
HO HAHAHAAHAHAA
HEE—hear

them now.
Reruns. Side
kicks. So riddle

this, Batman—
with the water
in your tank rising

risen, the sharks
unfed, slandered
& anxious

what tricks lie up
your mask? what
geniusy grab-bag

will you open
after this word
from our sponsor?

LINK PARABOLE

Now back
to our show, to our
question marks & fish

hooks—what
suffering shark
repellent

Batty, what holy
torpedoes
will rescue you

high, dry?

90. Nature Morte   { 1988 }

KING PLEASURE—
a crown drawn
over the ING—

be, pie, see, th—
all good ends
deserve begin

nings. His success
is ful—
remorse, mourn,

thank. It's the last
inning, winning
run on third

—so what's
the hitch?
Hooked

on phonics, canvas
orange as caution,
slow—treading light

ly—His days
lettered, spelt
out. Counted

like syll
-ables, -ogisms. Votes.
Vetos. Give us the dirt,

the pudding-proof—
child-, fire-, fool-
—keeping up

with his jonesing.
It's all Greek
to him—alpha

omega—paint
turning to words
& worry.

We want the scoop
the skinny—
this jig on a jag

269

the nig who would
be king.
Who can B

trust? -ed, mis-,
-worthy—
he's been written out

& off. Pronounce-
d dead. MOST YOUNG
KING GET THEIR

HEAD
CUT OFF. Here
is the low

down deal
the dope—Full
of tions

(*read:* shuns)—
situ-, tempta-
frustra-

—he be all
suffix, all after
& -likes—

life, child, dis, un

474.   This beautiful blue is to be arrested if the steel is suddenly taken out of the heat and buried in ashes. The blue steel works are produced in this way. If, again, the steel is held longer over the fire, it soon becomes a light blue, and so it remains.

—JOHAN WOLFGANG VON GOETHE
Theory of Colours

91. Light Blue Movers   { 1987 }

This tag not
to be removed.
Fit

to be tied
& gagged—
B rages

tossing
his cookies,
his art out

the window—
THE WHOLE
LIVERY LINE

BOW WITH THIS—
Basquiat case
bouncing off walls

padded with paintings
done in
his 8 hundred dollar

straitjacket
& tie—LUCKY
TO HAVE MY CANVAS SUIT

DRYCLEANED
BEFORE THE RIOTS.
He's ruint

—?;#@*!?!—
another pinstripe Armani
another painting

forsaken—not
for sale—
defenestrated. LIKE THIS

THE BIG MONEY
ALL CRUSHED—
Neighbors drag

some works in out
the rain—washed
up—salvaged

from his hip
wreck. Some show
up, days later,

at his dealer—
ALL CRUSHED
INTO THESE

FEET. Full
of bile, black,
yellow

—ill-humored—
his blood
Type A, boiling

like seas. EDGE
NOT REWORKED—Boy
Friday on Island

Manhattan (sold
for twentysome
clams & a handshake)

made USA. He's gone
from 100 Prince
to Great

Jones (right
above Bond), left
far behind his first dealer

& her basement
where, drugged up,
he worked—one day leaving

her no note, just
unfinished canvases
slashed like tires—steeling

himself—THESE FEET—the hood
ornament on a Cadillac
some swift, unseen

fingers freed.

93. Portrait of the Artist as a Young Derelict

CHEESE POPCORN

Down-
town & out
of it, found

by Haring, shot
laying on a grate—
B flat

on his back
—beat—
his last leg.

THE MENS SHELTER

ON THIRD—
tells Haring
he's about to head

west or south
—somewhere
sun shines,

some cliché.
SALT. MORTE.
Boho hobo—

he be easy
money. Pro
bono. Well, boys,

you both have made it—
have it made—
crashed

the party—opened Pop
Shops & slummed
at the Ritz.

45 RPM.
BLACK CHERRY
SODA. A LOT

OF BOWERY
BUMS USED
TO BE EXECUTIVES—

Now he's worn
out like shoes,
no support—dogs

so kicked
you gotta lie down
to get them on—

ANKLE exposed.
THIS BUM NAMED
BALTIMORE. A VAGRANT

NAMED CHICAGO—
no shelter,
plenty shade. DIS-

POSSESS NOTICE.
Refuse,
refugee—he all

dressed down
& no one
to be.

PLAID

PROSTITUTES—SON
OF A BUISNESS MEN
PLAYING CLARINET

FOR PORK AND BEANS
PLAID PLAID PLAID
PLAID PLIAD PLAID PLA

QUITE SURE. TKO
CROONERS. MAUI.
PLAID PLAID PLAID

PLAID PLAID PLAID
PLAID PLAID LARD
LARD—OR LATER—

WESTERN DIET OF
SETTLERS IN MOVIES
WAS BEANS, MOSTLY

LARD.   SMOKE RINGS
LONG HISTORY
FIVE CENT. TWO CENT.

BOOM BOOM—NUMBER
ONE. PLAID PLAID
PLAID PLAID PLAID

TRAIN TRACKS
BUILT BY MEN
OF CHINA FOR

CHUMP CHANGE
OF 1850—OR LATER—
LARD LARD—

NO DICE.
ORPHAN. PLAID
PLAID PLAID PLAID

FABRIC—INFESTED

GREENISH SKIN

GOOD PICTURE. Do not
adjust— envious
of his old

delf, B in
this alley in elegant
greenface—

GUMBY IS
BAD. Leprechaun,
leper, con

artist—
B witched,
standing beside

his portrait done in
mixed media
(i.e. piss & rust) by Warhol—

blown up
from a Polaroid—
headshot not

ACTUAL SIZE—
larger than life, paranoid,
keloid-covered—

smoking. Bogarted.
Boogeyman.
SHOULD BE ORANGE—

his hair shorn
à la Samson
FOLD BACK BRAIDS

PASS RING OVER
CABLE—
collie-cropped

neutered. Good
boy. Neutron
positron—INSIDE

THE PANEL
COVER. A pillar
of society—SALT—

graffitied on, divides
this frame—
F-TYPE (OPTIONAL)

TO VHF—his
PICTURE tube
of health blown—

fuzzy, like a security
cam or hospital
heartbeat—traces,

exposure, ghost images.

94. Oreo   { 1988 }

Split open
like a lip,
a pea

colored back
ground—
cream stuck

to one side
tongue turnt
to dark—TRICK

BLACK SOAP.
The mouth washed out—
Unlock

the Magic®—
dipped in milk.
Coconut. White

in hands, black
devoured last—
Teeth cleaned

like fish. Licked.

95. Calcium   { 1988 }

Cream. Men huddled
fortified. Half
& half. Atom

sign. Nucleus
meiosis—water
melond rind.

Smile. Coonskin
coat. White out. Winter.
TRANSMITTER—

Tyger Tyger
burning butter.
Lactate

intolerant. Litmus test.
Expiration date.
SUBJECT.

MILKSICKNESS—skim
whole, Duds.
Dairy trucks

colliding, bottles
broken. Don't cry—
condensed evaporated

dry homogenized.
Mixing milk
& melon can kill.

Put out
to pasteur—
Quart cartons

of lost children.

96. Victor 25448   { 1987 }

Let B = infinity

PUNCH INHIBIT
UNIT SHIFT
This is Only

A Test
User-
friendly Must fix

Crash
System error
Not enough memory

To complete
Operation
Conjunction

Junction
What's yr
Malfunction?

BLUEBIRD
BLUEBIRD
VICTOR

Hooking up
Phrases
& Negroes

& Robots—
Gone for a spin
For sale six gramophones

WAX WAX
WAX
"His Master's Voice"

Hambone
Hambone
Where you been—

IDEAL.
Automaton
Android

CUT OUT
Does not
Compute—

Heart a time
Bomb, ticks,
Takes licking, stutters

WORKS
Arms spoons
Being heated

Joints rusty
AXLE
A nail

And if that
Mockingbird
Don't sing

Momma's gonna
Buy you
A diamond ring,

Some rock—
A BEATING
AWAITS YOU

HERE
x's for eyes
SIZE

OF BUTTONHOLE—
Birds
circle his head

DESPUES D'UN PUÑO
Please Stand By
Repeat

This Is Only
ICARUS
ESSO

"Gentleman
We can
Rebuild him"

If I only had a brain
Start yr engine!
Six million

Dollar
Faster Better
Stronger

Grafting Skin
—human, living—
Onto a BIONIC©

281

Mainframe
"FLOORMOUNTED
EQUIPMENT"

Time Lapse
Lab Demo
Dramatization—

A fortune
In spare parts
MONEY

ORDERS
Model dis-
continued

Batteries Includead
This Message
Will Self-

Destruct in 5 seconds
Freak-a-zoids
Robots

Please report—
Save Delete
Nukeular Test Sight

All our operators
Standing by
We rejoin our regular

Five Four Three
Push to Stop
Pull to Run

Two One
Ground Zero
NOTHING

TO BE
GAINED HERE—
Already

In Progress

97. The Mechanics That Always
Have a Gear Left Over   { 1988 }

Horse-back
in the photograph,
on the wagon

again, wearing
a grin & one
of those fake Foreign

Legion hats,
flaps in the back
against the heat. Have-

locks. Gone
to Hawaii to kick
his habit & not

the bucket—
wasted not
wants not.

Brought
an expedition of free-
loaders, given

away, as Papa
would say, the store.
VENTA

TOTAL—
the sharking
shore—

THE WHITENESS
OF THE WHALE
AFFADAVIT CHART

JONAH HISTORICALLY
CONSIDERED—
The lone negro

on a lifeboat
—moral center—MONKEY
ROPE—go ask Canada

Lee or Jo. Singleton
Copley—
SHARK SHARK

SHARK SHARK.
His crew
has struck gold,

land, lightning.
Jackpot. Wind
fall. WHY

THE THUNDERBOLT KILLS
A DOES NOT
WOUND HIM—

They've held on
for the ride
of Frankenstein.

A made man.
TWIN STAR
RACING STYLE

TWIN SEAT TWIST
OF TOBACCO—
He gives

good bank.
FREE
(FOR A LIMITED

TIME ONLY).
His nature
nurtures—

green leaving
his hands
WHITE GLOVES

NO. 73
faster
than fingernails.

Don't matter—
another day,
another drawing

sold—failed sketches
found crumpled
in his trash—rifled

through, picked,
auctioned off. High
bidder. LABORATORY

TESTED
FOR STRENGTH
MOUTH TESTEDd

FFO   R
ESTHETICS.
Sick

of the bloody
city—man
overboard—SHARK

SHARK SHARK.
Only oils draw
him back—stretched

on linen, covering
it all, almost
"ANY BROKEN COIL"

with a blue
so sky
he could stay there—

98. To Be Titled

Once mild-
mannered
James Whathaveyou

till the bug, radio-
active, got hold him
GOOD ROAD

TO CHOOSE
turned him to Jimi
Hendrix Man,

COOL IRON.
"KING IS SHOWN
W/ TALL CROWN

AND GOATEE."
Southpawed
his way to the top,

high above
the crowd—FLESH.
SPIRIT. HOT

IRON. TUMBLING
HORSESHOES—
Hendrix backing Lil'

Richard's Band,
Hendrix in Electric
Ladyland—

LONE RANGER—
remakes hisself
& our Star Spangled

feedback—panic—
the rockets red
blare, the bombs

burning like hair—

wordless, whiplash.
Voodoo Chile folds the world
like a flag, a losing

hand HAWKMAN. Gone
from Experience
to Band

of Gypsy's—
ROAD SPOILED
PLAYED OUT

BY OTHER HOBOS—

BIG DRUM. The ax
raised behind
his back—he licks

a six-string
of hits—head
bands, trips—

put ons, come
ons, coming
down— NEE NAH

UNBREAKABLE
LIFE GUARANTEE—
he downs

horse pills, handful,
to sleep.
ARSENIC.

DANGEROUS
DRINKING WATER—
On fire, burns

his guitar in effigy, self-
immolation,
IMMORTALITY©.

100. Riding with Death   { 1988 }

The bit
of bones beneath
him, reined—

he mounts
Death
's bleached back—

a brown body out-
lined on linen.
SPINE. TORSO. SIN

HUESO. He's
too through
with this merry-

go-round—the clowns—
the giant stuffed
animals to win

or take your picture
with—the pony rides
& overpriced

food. *There's always
a unicycle.*
His hands turned

forks, tuning,
feeding what hunger
held him together

this long. Trawling
his own stomach.
Tripe. The snipe hunt

he's begun has come
up empty—left holding
the bag—trick,

nickel—this cat's
gotten out, crossed
the path. Curious—

his horse
turned back

from our foxhunt,

this possum run.
Given in—SAMO©
AS AN ESCAPE

CLAUSE—found face
down
like a payment.

And we who for ages
whaled, blubber
& wonder

why he's thrown
ashore, rowed
himself here

hallelujah—answered
out the blue
whale some unseen

call. A siren—
the ambulance
racing a sea

of cars—*emergency*—
family only
beyond this

point—our fists
against his breath-
less chest.

101. Will (& Testament)

Leave
nothing
unsaid

102. Kalik   { 1988 }

If not caught
jumping
a turnstile, shot

in the back by a cop,
then the end gets us
DEATH OF MARAT

at home—
most accident happen
in bathroom—

ALUM
SAND BORAX
AERIAL URINE—

tub filled warm
eyes empty
& open armed

to see into the blue
that covers
EYE OF TROOF

the whole picture—
pen mid-
sentence, death

in the quill
raised or fallen
flat & still, we will

note surprise & then
say how paint
predicts—when

becomes the only quest-
ion. BASEHEAD 1960
FERMENTATION.

GERMAN GERMAN
POISON. Wearing
blue, his force

field's down, cloaking
device off—DANCING
WAX FIGURES

DANCING WAX—This far
in space exploding
stars make no sound

& it takes
quite a while for their
light to reach down—

103. Eroica   { 1988 }

BEAM: TO LOOK
BEAN: TO SUN
BAT: AN OLD OLD

WOMAN
MAN DIES.
MAN DIES.

AIRCOOLED
CONDENSER
BAGPIPE: 1940s

VACUUM CLEANER
B.O.A.C : BUREAU
OF DRUG ABUSE

CONTROL
BALE OF STRAW: WHITE
BLOND FEMALE

BALL & CHAIN: WIFE
BALLOON ROOM:
PLACE WHERE

MARIJUANA IS SMOKED
MAN DIES. MAN
DIES. MAN DIES.

BALLS: TESTICLES
BAM: (FROM BAMBITA)
BANANA: ATTRACTIVE

LIGHT SKIN
BLACK FEMALE
BAND: WOMAN

BAND: JAZZ
BANG: INJECTION
OF NARCOTICS

OR SEX.
MAN DIES.
BANJO: INSTR

FRM WEST
AFRKA

293

BANK: TOILET

TNT
(—6H2 CH)
MORNING GLORY

SWEET POTATO
MAN DIES.
MAN—

FOR BLUES
FIXIN TO DIE
BLUES

BARK: HUMAN SKIN

You can see lots of self-fulfilling prophesies in his work, or in the work of anybody whose work runs deep. I don't think Andy did the *Last Supper* because he planned to die. I don't think Jean did the *Man Dies* painting in his last show because he planned for that to be his last show. He loved to live, as you can tell. But maybe the more you love it and the better you do it the more resistance you encounter. Especially if you work all the way.

Creating his last show was an ordeal for him because he wasn't well and he was in an almost paranoid state about the serious "dis" that he was getting from certain quarters of the art world. Lots of people wanted him to fall. It made me sick. I can only imagine how he felt. But his sick was better than most people's well, and the last time I dreamed about him he said he was felling [sic] much, much better.

—GLENN O'BRIEN

104. TV Star   { 1988 }

2 NEWS

Such poor
reception—double
exposure—deals—

thank God you're not
here. Canceled—
no more seasons

or sweeps, just dust
gathering on a blue screen.
Spared. Edited

for content. Haven't,
down on luck, gone & done
1-900-GET-BSQT—

your own Blk Psychic
Sex Hotline
Enterntainment Only—

Instead you star-
red in the Jones
—Rev'nd Jim—

Story made
for TV—formatted
to fit your screen—

lined up to take the Kool
Aid—red zip
coon smile

on the packet—
sipping the poison
slow—for God's

sake—Dramatization
adapted
from actual events—

adjusted to run
in time allotted—
~~FOOL~~ in a far-

off country—

11 WEBSTER

Little man,
what made you
think you'd make it

big? DORIAN
HAREWOOD
CH. 2, 12:40 AM

You're in a short
list of us—Jet's
Beauty of Week

or People
Are Talking About…
out of sync

touch, unfocused
or over-
exposed—

Plaything
to the Stars…
You've sang & sat

on more laps
than Hollywood
strip-

pers. Johns
here are half
dead—Live

Live Girls—
dollar bills
placed thin

in your faux-
foaming,
famished mouth—

MAGNUM

In studio
photo beside
himself

& African
drums, a pop
gun play-pointed

BLUEBIRD
BLUEBIRD
VICTOR

at his head
like some Prince
—Freddy, that is—

Chico without
the Man, coked
up, checking out

DIABLO
GIN; DITTO
SM AS ABVE—

he's eyed & bleary
ADD. PROOF
—a wounded horse

begging for to be shot

THEE'S COMPANY

God & he deep
in conversating—
OSCILLOSCOPE

PASSPORT (VERSION)
FLSH BULB—
The light goes on

Then off—
BELL; BUZZER
—this land

Lord want his rent.
Pay up
—HOTEL—

Or else. "POOR BEN"—
time to collect
that severance

Check—garnished
wages of sin. Early
retirement, honorable dis-

Charge, he been given
only this lousy
gold-plated watch

—A fake—
whose hands
run always late

AMBER VISION

DEFLECTS
ULTRA
VIOLET RAYS

*S *EE*
*N
*E*E*I*IO*

3 ROOM
$189
MULTICOLORED

LONG W RING
          EA
UV-400

BLOCKS
HARMFUL
RAYS

SPEEDY

Before you can say
Jack Robinson
no sooner than the words

Speedy Gonzales leave
the lips
he upped

like an ante
& went.
Andelé! Andelé!

Arriva! left us
in the dust
the road. *If he catches*

you you're through—
the sombrero,* the grin
of cheese** won't save you

*or the straw-hat
from the Islands
[where that?]

**or the time mugging
for Warhol, huge fake
ears on, eyelids flipped

up, out, nose flared
as if some cartoon
animal froze-frame—

Wile E. Coyote, SUPER
GENIUS. Trailing smoke accent-thick—
no good—lazy—he stays

in his mouse-
hole all day,
barely a peep

—*meep meep*—grins
like the cat that ate
canary.† [†Tweety.]

Not him—outwits
the predators & traps
or least out-talks

& leaves his zorroed mark—
transparent pages
[known as cels]

drawed on—that, if turned
fast enough,
make like motion—

SOAPS

Due to illness
abrupt, the part
of Johnny will be

played by Tony
Award Winner©
Jeffrey Wright

—understudy, cue
card. Carte blanche.
And action! Lines learnt

in one day.

Will Johnnyboy
recover from his long

sickness his fights
with father?
His mother the institution

leave? Stay
tuned the next
Guiding—The Price

is Right—all this
week on As the World—
makeovers + amnesiacs

+ sons who want
tell our viewers
We've made it!

We're no longer high
school ugly duckings
We're no longer—

And now this word
—99 44/100 pure—
The plot thickens

like blood, hard
to get out—colors
may run bleed fade—Try

now + save—if not
satisfied fully—toll
free—simply return—

PLEDGE DRIVE

Canned, can-
celed mid-season—
his show has hit

the road, the drawing
board, barely
past the pilot. Turned

to telethon—
something begging
something once

301

a year to pledge.
Operators
standing by—may

cause drowsiness
cancer causing
agents—Every

bit little helps.
Reruns
(none) & no

syndication—he's on
his own devices
—for a price—

biopic-ed off. Where
what
is he? History

105. Haiku

*after Jean-Michel
Basquiat*

piggy
bank
ride

drive-by
shoe-
in

culture
shock
treatment

sid viscous

bank
fortune
teller

mock
turtle
soup

to
be
continued

106. The Pictures

ADVANCE PUBLICITY FOR THE FILM
VERSION OF THE LIFE & TIMES
OF JEAN-MICHEL BASQUIAT
AS DIRECTED BY JULIAN SCHNABEL

He's hot!
He's black!
He   dead!

ART HOUSE REVIVAL

Intro'd
from the dark
continent—African

Killer B—deadly—
wrapped
mystery—the Living

Mummy! Scarabs
scabs. He's back!
like you never

seen him before!
haunting, cursed
—the mask

beneath the MGM
Lion—brown
with a wide

white mouth.
The CBS eye.
In his own life

story, he plays
hisself. "CREATURE
FROM BLACK

LAGOON." washed up,
B movie star
sludges ashore—

Night
of the Living,
Men from Outer

Mars—Badder
than ever, Dracula's
Soul Brother.

Zombie
—or werewolf—
half man

half aminal
he sprouts hair
even underground

—Ends This Week!—
even days
later, after, in the grave.

THE LATE SHOW

The dead don't
miss us—the dead
miss movies—

licorice darkness,
that salt popcorn
kiss, cool assurance

of blank screens—
black
hat versus white,

cowboying
that hypnotic road
so quick we don't

know we're moving.
Matins, matinees—
the dead hate

their new, subtitled
lives—love
scenes read, a car

chase translated—
The dead have waited
in the john

or ladies lounge
long enough, stuck
in the harsh flourescent

of between—
want to sneak
back in

the picture—
Shhhhh
Thank You

Not Smoking—
angry at
the tireless

Usher
who scoured the aisles
flashlit & kicked

them out just
when they'd propped
their feet. No more

previews, no
newsreels or shorts
stinging like salt

the hands.
For restricted
audience only—

FIN & then
the roles roll
by—assigned

like plots,
graves. Special thanks.
Soundtrack avail.

©MCMLXXXVIII.

Any resemblance
to persons living
or dead coincidence—

lights resurrect—
the egress
like regrets, lit clear.

107. Two Photographs
of Jean-Michel Basquiat, Paris

1988

Face all
tore up
from the smack

he's stark
staring
clutching Kerouac

to his chest—
The Subterraneans
edition as beat

up as he looks. His last

show & promo—
around his neck
the bolero—

its boxer getting
licked, strung
out, face giving way

DESPUES DE UN PUÑO

or his own fist
raised
in defense

defiant—laced
tight. Arm up
like a slot

machine's—BAR
BAR BELL—he's hit
jackpot, his eyes

have it—looking
something
like starlight

(far-off, half-
dead already)
hand covering one eye.

1986

Bare
chested, the noose
like a Texas string-tie

casual, loose—
black
tie affair. Lasso

lariat, he's at
the end
of his yoke—

pulling the horse
before being carted
off. Monkeying

around. He's both
the tree—banyan
or baobab—

& the hanging
man. Gallows
humor. Tongue-

tied. One day his luck
will run out
like his friends—

let's hope long after the dope does—

close call, cropped
hair—suppose he dries up,
then out, gets

clean & finds God—

Let us help
him sip *café*
au lait, laughing

beside the still waters.

108. Pentimento

Old paint on canvas, as it ages, sometimes becomes transparent. When that happens it is possible, in some pictures, to see the original lines: a tree will show through a woman's dress, a child makes way for a dog, a large boat is no longer on an open sea. That is called pentimento because the painter "repented," changed his mind. Perhaps it would be as well to say that the old conception, replaced by a later choice, is a way of seeing and then seeing again.

—LILLIAN HELLMAN
Pentimento

DOS CABEZAS 2

We are the walking
wounded in war
movies who insist

Go head
without us—
so on

youse went—

Now we forget
what the fight
was for first

place—ANTONIUS SEPTIMUS
FIRE OF CARNIUS
ASCETICISM—Last leg

of the relay
race & medals weight
down our chests

without a limb
to pin them with.
HOMER

ILIAD TROY
ACHILLES—
You are a ghost

itch, the knee we
no longer have
& have

learned to live
without. What we bare-
ly miss. Being

behind is sometime
worse, the survivor
's curse

& cure: remember…

MAN STRUCK LIGHTNING—
2 WITNESSES

Hell is no help.
Here, unharrowed,
hurried, you are before

your time, some
sacrifice up in flame—
lamb, lion, monkey

up a tree.
You're early. We
still run on

CPT—taking
sweet our time
—form a single line—

getting around
to you—
Your mama.

Thou art
in the ante-
chamber of after

—the Big Below—
downtown in this
City of Dis

where your ears
from our words
must burn—

ANYBODY SPEAKING WORDS

Nothing can breathe
you back. Not
the long work

of drink, cocktails
at six, beer,
whatever, whisky,

Old Granddad, Crazy-
horse. SPORTS. The dull
sweet white wine taste

of morning. Nor
the eastward walk
past St Mark's

& Auden's marked
house, past
the park, skip

rope of streets no longer
numbers, into the Nix
the Nada—to cop

the coin-sized, -colored
bags. Squats. The poor
tarred
streets, corners piled

with boys & beggars.
Smoke smoke. OPERA.
Your faraway father

in his suit
coat of silence. Your mouth
mock-moving on

its own. NOTHING
TO GAIN HERE. Gone,
nothing can stir—

ERNOK

AWOL, SNAFU, VIP
You done
been abbrev'd—

sent into the DMZ
history—
RIP, VFW

BFD—bearing
left, nitro-
glycerine

in yr trunk
TNT, FDA
you pkged yourself

special 4th
class rate
snuck past the drug

sniffing dogs
at Bureau Tobacco
& Firearms

under siege
the influence.
Stamped rec'd.

COD. JFK. MLK. BOOSH-
WAH-ZEE OR CIA?
You come to us piece

meal—LSD, AC
DC, BCBG, OD,
DOA—under cover

the mask the gun
to produce—
BSQT 83, JMB

on the hook
the take. NFS. HNIC.
MOMA, CBGB'S—

it's anyone's guess
what all
you stand for. PS—

remittance req'd
w/in 30 days
RSVP ASAP

"REPLICAS"

And after all this
time, guess who
decides to show

up—through—
your paint
thinning as you

once feared
—as your hair never did—
the head behind

CHKN appearing,
the face beneath
the halo—pentimento—

going the way
of nothing else on earth:
returns. CAST IRON

AUTOMOBILE REPLICAS.
You are ex-
cavated, communicated—

the faces pressing
from beneath the painting
—X-RAY GLASSES—

giving a glance
of what's past.
DRY GOODS

ACTUAL SIZE
NEGRO SPIRITUALS—
What the ghost wants

is not always
obvious—knocks
as if it knows

who's hidden
or why—please, one
momento mori—

*AY ALLAH ENLA*G* Y*U
M*Y ZEUS E*LARGE YO*
        BUDDAH EN*A*GE *OU—

Better this life—grief—
beyond death
than the death-in-life—

GRI GRI

You are what
's missing—
the spook we have

not seen—haint
haunting
—what's that—

STERILE DESTROY
AFTER SINGLE
USE. No matter

what vévé
we make, what
tobey we take

as totem, the b-b-
bogeyman gonna
get us—some spirits,

like likker, never rest.
If only
the left side

of the equation were
true: what does not
make you stronger

will kill you. Go ask
the vermin behind
the fridge—nuclear

survivors, roach
motel fine diners—
this house falling

around you—the mice—
no piper to pay or play—
poltergeists rattling

their chains like dice—

109. Soul

Given up
a life
of falsetto

fuzzy hats
& funk
soundtracks

to find God—
Rev Green
on the good foot

gone back
to singing the gospel
before soul—

sanctified—baptized
by a pot
of boiling grits

grafted to his skin—
pressed—re-issued
from the original

masters—Aretha
Franklin & blind
black musicians—

both Ray & Wonder.
Praise
the Lord & please

give to the Fraternal
Order
of Wheelchair-Bound
Black Singers

—a moment of silence—
Pres. Curtis Mayfield
& Teddy

Pendergrass, Vice-
—gone is the life
of ladies'

panties thrown
like a voice
onstage, going

gold. Pledge now
to the Association
of Shot

Soul Singers
& Last Words
—Sam Cooke, founder—

Bitch, you shot me

slumped in a chair.
What's going on?
What's going on? Co-

founder Marvin Gaye gunned
down by God—
his father

the right reverend—
the son—holy—*O*
Mercy Mercy Me—

poor Donny Hathaway
five stories
up, mistaking plain air for

a walk across water

110. The Ninth Circle

In a back booth
Mingus, Chas. is upset
    that Lenny Bruce

keeps using the word *cunt*
    in this his last act, uncut—
Mingus sitting up front

    with the critics, the shrinks
who each set and session
    hand him drugs—he's checked

hisself into Bellevue,
    a ward without
any way out. *All the Things You*

Could Be by Now
    If Sigmund Freud's
Wife Was Your

Mother. The thick haze
    of Camels and buddha—
The Black Saint & the Sinner Lady—

    in this halfway house
to heaven. *Oh Lord Don't Let*
    Them Drop that Atom

Bomb on Me. He's the life
    of the after party, setting
like a jet, slapping that upright

    till he bleeds—onstage, caps
on other player's bits—
    You got no tone—scats

and bangs the piano with his fist.
    They didn't teach us to talk,
says Mingus. He's not pissed, just

    paces, speaking a blues streak.
Puffs a pipe, intellectual-
    like, blowing smoke

shooting off his rifle
    —the kind that killed
Kennedy—like a mouth. *This mule*

could be called
stubborn & lazy
            But in a clever sort

of way, this mule could be
            waitin & learnin & plannin
for a sacred kind of day—

            SEMI CIRCLE OF DAMNATION.
DIGESTIVE TRACT.
            CIRCULATORY SYSTEM. PAN-

LUNARISM. Evicted
            from the Great Jones school
he built and planned—

            his cool
has gone—cries
            as his bookcases and dreams pile

along the curb. *My country*
            Tis of Thee, Sweet
Land of Slavery—

            Mingus thanks the cops,
says he thinks
            they're trying to help

as they put him in the cruiser, booked
            for unknown pills, blues,
an empty syringe. No dope. Onlook

            as the city reposesses
the beds and books,
            even his bass

            put under lock—
Mingus cracking up, in pieces
            like chess. Rooked.

Onstage wearing his African "dress"
            Mingus wields
the neck of his bass

            like a bottle—
a fifth
            of gin—or a battle

axe. *The Shoes*
    Of the Fisher-
Man's Wife Are Some Jive Ass

Slippers.   Before
    Lou Gehrig's disease
grounds him, Mingus's fingers blister

    Better Git It in Your Soul and *Please*
Come Back from the Moon—
    finding that note, exact, his upright's

full bodied, unbowed, half-human moan.

111. Epitaph

You done blown
this taco stand
sky high, AMF

under earth,
an oath. Caught
the first thing

smoking. PARA
MORIR. Gone
with summer-

time
& the living
is easy. High

cotton.
You weevil
why'd you

weave us?
Stitch yourself
back like a spider

or under-
taker—
give up the car

service that waits
& waits while you
paint—it's too

much—will drive
you to your grave.
DEC 1960

AUG 1988—
your date
kept, no chance

to grow fat
& useless—no
names please—

GREENWOOD.
You stay
thin & dead, a language—

maggot:
n. 2. *an extravagant
notion, whim*—ants

for angels, eyes—

The artist's grave, however, conjures up his collectors' greatest fear, the anonymity that threatened to be Basquiat's fate....It is virtually impossible to find, located near the center of Green-Wood Cemetery, where Brooklyn has buried its dead for more than a century, overlooking New York Harbor, with Manhattan in the far distance. The headstone, marked JEAN-MICHEL BASQUIAT, ARTIST, DEC 1960 AUG 1988, is barely eight inches high, and is flanked by those of two other Brooklynites, named Russo and DeLorenzo. But for the inscriptions, they are indistinguishable, as indentical as the bricks lining a garden. The inexpensive plot isn't exactly potter's field, but neither does it seem remotely like a shrine to a fallen genius.

—DAVID D'ARCY

112. Shrine Outside Basquiat's Studio, September 1988

Back on Great
Jones
his face

against the façade
fronting the carriage
house rented

from Warhol—
inside, his suits
stiffen from starch,

spilt paint.
He's bought
the farm whole,

enchilada
& all—August
& the heat

covering everything,
needle-sharp,
asleep. No more

feeding
his habit art—
he's gone

& done it
this time, taken
his last dive.

Exit, stage right.
A broken
record—his black

skin thick,
needled
into song—

a swan's. Upon
graffitied brick—
INSIDIOUS MENACE

LANDLORD
TENANT—
folks pile

candles flowers
photos notes
to God & lace—

anything TO REPEL
GHOSTS, keep
his going at bay

before memory comes
early, snarling
& sweeps him

into the mouth
of euphemism—
sanitation worker, waste

management engineer,
garbage man, dumpster
diver, trash

heap, heaven.

113. Vanitas

The best *vanitas* paintings contradict themselves. They purport to teach us the emptiness and impermanence of worldly objects while infusing them with transcendent significance and giving them relative permanence.

The modern implication of conceit now associated with the word *vanity* is not present in the use of *vanitas,* the Latin word for "emptiness."

—SALLY FISHER
The Square Halo

Without you we are
    only words
we manage

to get wrong—
    your name
a death

sentence mis-
    pronounced, u-
nanimous—

Since your lethal
    injection
we have you all

backwards,
    ward back
your zombie, trans

-posed, -lated—
    Even your tag
anagrams to SOMA

—South
    of Market—
the body—DRINK

OF THE GODS.
    Death
has found you

Cuban, victim
    of acronyms—
AIDS, FBI, CIA

OR BOOSH-WAH-ZEE?
　　Syllabic
symbolic, psuedonymous—

your name sticks
　　with us like Malcolm
Ten, or freeze tag

—you're it—
　　kicking cans
playing graveyard. In this grey

game of telephone
　　you are on
the fritz—the lam

—*911*—dis
　　-connected,
-missed.

Asleep
　　you count
black sheep

bah, bas-
　　relief—
receding with each

touch. Our
　　sweat spoils
your face. You are what

we say of saints,
　　assumed—
Your name, mis

-placed, -took
　　echoes
about the room.

114. Relics

> He had to live up to being a young prodigy,
> which is a kind of false sainthood.
> —KEITH HARING

THRONE

See his chair
everywhere—
first against

the wall or
beneath René
Ricard's portrait—

THE GREAT UNWASHED
GOTHIC PAINTING
BLEACHED ASSASSIN CURATES

MILAGE OVER A DISTANCE—

B money
squatting, in color
—UNBREAKABLE—

it's there
in the corner, the throne
not yet torn

SLAPPING SENSE
IN TERMS OF TICKING
SUITCASES

DENIES EVER SEEING—

crouched yellow
& black beneath
canvases waiting

to be covered.
KING PLEASURE
leans the wall

besides @#$%&*!!
an axe.
In Basquiat's

hands a cigarette
lit, a cup—
paint—

raised to drink,
bless. Toast.
ZZZZZZZ ZZ Z—

Hard to believe
this is where
he once thought & drew—

BRONZE THIS HIGH
BRICK INLAY
EYES IN ANGRY

TO BE ANSWERED—

breath, but here it is
—a fact—& when
no one looks

we sit ourselves & wait

CRAVAT

"Looks like something
you'd clean
your shoes with"

says Our Lady
of Belfast, of Constant
Shyness & she's

right—the tie
that never bound
his neck, bought only

to trade with the assistant
behind Mary
Boone's desk,

is ugly as sin.
Mud-brown, grey,
with red veins

strip-mined down—
it's neither thin
nor wide, time-

less, dated.
MISSONI
UOMO

MADE
WOOL—
price tag still

on, expensive
even now, this tie
points downtown

MANO
MANO
SOHO—

could we still
return this thing
if we want?

MOHAIR
IN SPAIN—
Worn

only once
by the assistant
when he swapped

his tie with Ste
Jean-Michel
of the Perpetual

Deal, Patron
of Paint
& Derelicts,

who in turn took
—looped—the assistant's
bright silk

for a belt—

LOVE

Pink ladies—
a half-gallon
of blues—

large horse-pills
some say add
up to love—

hard to swallow
buy—most just grow
sleepy. A year's supply—

he owns in a jar more
than the city had
before the drought began—

Now love
is a canal, a con-
taminated place—

a word found
on a fridge he painted
when younger

& a smart
someone saved it, took
the door off

to sell—now none will
climb inside
what's left behind

& have it close like
a kiss
or a coffin

BRAIN©

Upstairs,
     Superfly loops on,
          watching the room—

nobody home. *I'm your mama
     I'm your daddy*—
          Basquiat's 57 Jones

329

Street pad stands empty
        like a tomb
                pirated. *Tell ole*

Pharoah, let my people go.

Laboratory
        lobotomy—
                he's cooking

with grease, his
        brain pickled
                as if a mummy's

(pulled out slowly, bit
        by bit, with a hook
                then stored

honeyed, in small jars).
        Shine
                sir? on his knees

yassah yassah
        painting—
                HEAD

OF A FRYER
        SARCOPUGUS
                OF A PHYSICIAN.

The boot
        black stand
                piled high upon

the grey
        matter of boxes,
                color xeroxes—

The sign
        for salt
                —a tesseract—

drawn on a soap
        box. PODIUM. SUB
                COMMUNICATOR—

Upstairs, Priest wants
        out of the Life
                giving up

white women & fur
   for piece
      of quiet. ONE WOMAN'S

MAN. A YOUTH
   WITH "CROW" SYNDROME:
      (AN ATTRACTION

TO SHINY OBJECTS),
   Little plastic men
      with parachutes, LPs

line the room—
   HUMAN ANATOMY.
      WORLD HISTORY.

PARADE/RIOT.
   HUMAN HEART
      HUMAN HEART™

Packrat, pickup
   artist—
      he's saved everything

cept hisself.
   NEW CONFESSIN' THE BLUES
      DEPRESSED PALSY TV—

By the time
   we find it, enter
      unknocked

like the PO-LEEECE
   —freeze—
      the place

has changed like a mind—
   someone tipped him
      off & our boy's split—

his magpie
   nest turned
      to cold storage

for vegetables—
   radishes & cabbage & Chinese
      noodles, dirt-brown potatoes

with one hundred eyes, winking.

ONE MAN SHOW

Apples, orangutans—
on Lafayette, below Shinbone
Alley, Basquiat is high

up, muraled, sprayed against
the scapula-shaped bldg
in his (now) famous

VanDerZee pose. (*Trans:*
"By the Sea.") Today the city
is someone familiar

round every corner.
*Spartacus 1960. Upper
View.* Brains

& radiant
babies in the No
Man's Land north

of Haring's Pop
Shop. *Never Eat
Pork: Their Golden Rule.*

This mural's garish
colors do not suit
but stay—least

longer than you
managed to. Apology
apostrophe—

you sit bored, called
for jury duty,
condemned—tenement

testament man.

CANONIZATION

You died days
before St John
the Baptist (his

beheading)
on a day of sun
sans music—a

capella—
you have joined
them, the patrons of ores

& Bohemia—
the ones with altars
& metals

& occassions.
St Martin
de Porres (interracial

justice & hair-
dressers)
who sold hisself again

& again to gain
money for the church—
able to appear

& disappear, power
of aerilization
(hence patron

saint of television)
would have been proud.
You are our St Ides

of March, that talk
behind
your back—

Et tu, Judas?

to which we
bow, reply, like Moses
the Black

of Abyssinia, dead
your same day
(Byzantine calendar)

born a slave, committed
the most heinous
crimes & then converted

(means not known).
Met by marauders
& martyred

when he would not save
himself by force—
"The Ethiopian Hermit"

known in his life
for his extreme
mortifications. DANGEROUS

NEIGHBORHOOD.
In what state
did you lay? How

long? DOUBTFUL
DOUBTFUL—Come,
let us pray.

Let us kneel to Benedict
the Moor, to all
the Black

Madonnas, let us kiss
the cross
of Crispus Attucks' arms—

115. Heaven   { 1985 }

Can we get
a Witness
Protection Pro-

gram like you
did? Sent
into hiding, secret

identity, altered
ego as if Clark
Kent. Don

some glasses & that
is that. AUTO-
PORTRAIT.

DEAD BIRD©.
Awww
next time Boss

you *play Superman—*

convince everyone
it's him committing
the crime, not you

on a diamond spree
trafficking—
him who's taken

wing—ASCENT
<u>FLESH</u>
SPIRIT

Geez Boss
it was only
a fin

(police whistle)

—Next time it'll be
a Mickey Fin.
You slipped

*U*ERMA*
duped & downed
like a drink.

Who'da think
you'd end up
amnesiac, new

name & no way
home? Under
our yellow sun

—class A star—
your powers
failed—up

up away—
too much krypt-
onite kept

in a lead box

even your X-
ray specs could not
penetrate

or name. CYCLOPS.
MOTIONLESS
AIR—MIRROR MASTER

ANOTHER
SATISFIED COMB
USER. Your cape

a shroud
a shrug—RIBBED
WING PARTLY

COVERED IN SILK—
in sky
bird plane

faster loco-
motive smoke.
A*ION COMIC*—

You're up
—& out—there
somewhere, making

it safe for all.
(NEGRO
SPANIARD). CRANK

like a call—
Can we
get a wit-

ness? VICE;
a President, something
votive to see

& save us, say,
spin the earth
alternate universe

Mr Mxyzptlk.
This piece of blue
kryptonite—or red—

has a diff. effect
each time. Bizarro—
SOJUZ PLODO

sometime you grow
six limbs—count—
others it strikes

you down, slow
—no Lois, no Jimmy
Olsen to pick

the lock & set
you free—Super-
dog, Supermonkey

Supercat & -horse—

who live on the moon.
HEAVEN©.
Can we get some

witness? Come on
into the shun sine
Superboy—

say something.
Anything. Spare
us this silence

—fortress solitude—
this invincible
bulletproof blue—

HENRY GEDZAHLER: *You got rid of your telephone a while ago. Was that satisfying?*

J-M BASQUIAT: Pretty much. Now I get all these telegrams. It's fun. You never know what it could be. "You're drafted," "I have $2,000 for you." It could be anything. And because people are spending more money with telegrams they get right to the point. But now my bell rings at all hours of the night. I pretend I'm not home…

—Making It New

116. Urgent Telegram to Jean-Michel Basquiat

HAVENT HEARD FROM YOU IN AGES STOP LOVE YOUR
LATEST SHOW STOP THIS NO PHONE STUFF IS FOR BIRDS
LIKE YOU STOP ONCE SHOUTED UP FROM STREET ONLY

RAIN AND YOUR ASSISTANT ANSWERED STOP DO YOU
STILL SLEEP LATE STOP DOES YOUR PAINT STILL COVER
DOORS STOP FOUND A SAMO TAG COPYRIGHT HIGH

ABOVE A STAIR STOP NOT SURE HOW YOU REACHED STOP
YOU ALWAYS WERE A CLIMBER STOP COME DOWN SOME
DAY AND SEE US AGAIN END

I met Jean-Michel Basquiat a few days before he died. Before or after, it doesn't really matter.

—Dany Laferrière

117. Retrospective

In the dark, the nasty
night, mother of million
nights, you return

looking, not for fame
but ducats, not begging
but collecting

on what was
owed you, getting back
what you sharked.

Lien.
Let us guess
JMB—you can see

everything clear
as your complexion,
as composed. COWARDS

WILL GIVE
TO GET RID
OF YOU. Even when

your skin gave in
to the heroin, you still
looked young & beautiful—

yet you confess
you feel much
better now, got

a handle on things,
the drugs fled on
out, left cold

turkey. THE SKY
IS THE LIMIT©.
Wings

& white meat.
Spleen still
missing, but not

quite missed.
If only
you'd said so

long like a television
station, signed off
the air—Star

Spangled Banner
blowing before bars—
red, yellow,

more—color—
before brief
black—the static—

LINER NOTES
ACKNOWLEDGMENTS
INDEX

Liner Notes

In treating Jean-Michel Basquiat's work and life—a distinction his so-called critics have often blurred—we have consulted many sources. A complete bibliography would be far too long & missing the point, especially for an artist who appropriated & copyrighted as many images & sayings as he created. Moreover, this is not a biography, but an extended riff—Basquiat and his work serves as a bass line, a rhythm section, a melody from which the poems improvise. I did not know Basquiat; I do now, through his work. Most important to a full grasp of his life, is to see his paintings live.

Some helpful references: The Whitney's *Basquiat*, edited by Richard Marshall; Henry Gedzahler's 1983 interview with the artist, found in *Making It New;* Vrej Barhoomian's black market *Basquiat*; Phoebe Hoban's "SAMO©...Is Dead: The Fall of Jean-Michel Basquiat"; and *Basquiat Drawings* & *Notebooks*, roughly in that order. Greg Tate's "Flyboy in the Buttermilk" is one of the earliest and still one of the best writings on Basquiat; of the growing number of articles on the artist since then, one from the British *Guardian* stands out as another balanced and accurate piece of journalism.

To give a visual idea of Basquiat's hand, SMALL CAPITALS generally indicate painted/drawn text found in his work. Titles often correspond to paintings; the dates following titles apply to the work and are included to indicate a sense of the history of the art & artist. (Dates are *not* the dates of my composition). Some might notice I have crossed out words and even a few track titles in the table of contents; of such crossings, Basquiat said, "I cross out words so you will see them more: the fact that they are obscured makes you want to read them." Likewise, rest assured that there are no typos or "misspellings" here—such alternative spellings are part of a vernacular, not accidental, but conscious and necessary. They are, in a sense, another kind of rewriting what we mean (and what is meant for us); they are spells of a larger sort. Basquiat, in the context of the seeming casualness of his canvases, put it best: "Everything is well stretched even though it looks like it might not be."

As might be expected, a show about Basquiat includes "found" text & imagery. The following list includes those things not common knowledge or property:

1. **Campbell's Black Bean Soup:** *for Ellen Gallagher.* The quote *a nigger's loft* taken from *The Andy Warhol Diaries*, ed. Pat Hackett.
2. **Poison Oasis:** To be read *al dente*, slowly.
6. **Vocabulario:** *for R.A.* By all reports, Basquiat spoke impeccable Spanish, having lived in Puerto Rico when younger.
7. **Bros. Sausage:** During one of his many attempts to run away from home, Basquiat went to a state park. He soon returned. See *Making It New.*
13. **Oleo:** Bert Williams ("Uncle Eggs"), famous light-skinded comedian who performed in blackface, the first black person in the Ziegfield Follies. "Wait till Martin comes," meaning Go Down, Death, quoted in *Harlem Renaissance.*
15. **New York/New Wave: THE WOLVES:** Malcolm McClaren, manager/producer of the Sex Pistols, also produced the new wave band Bow Wow Wow. Led by a teenage singer, the group produced hits & albums with provocative titles in the tradition of Sex Pistols but with a racial twist—*Jungle Boy, TV Savage, King Kong.*
17. **Times Square Show:** *for Richard E. in Nash.*
19. **Defacement:** Michael Stewart, graffiti artist, was killed by New York's finest for spray-painting in the subway.

24. **Amateur Bout.** Limited to 1000 shrinkwrap copies. Editorial & design supervision by Gerard Malanga.

27. **VNDRZ:** James VanDerZee, photographer, documented famous and local Harlem figures from the 1920s until his death in 1982, a year after he photographed Basquiat. His name means "by the sea."

29. **Jack Johnson:** In the voice of the first black heavyweight champion of the world, tried for "white slavery" under the Mann Act. For further reference, we suggest *Bad Nigger!*, his autobiography *Jack Johnson Is a Dandy, Jack Johnson & His Times*, and Arthur Ashe's *Hard Road to Glory*. Also "The Black Hamlet" from *Sports Illustrated*, 1959. Miles Davis recorded the score (& wrote liner notes) to the eponymous 1969 documentary, narrated by Brock Peters.

30. **Notary Public:** *for John Schlesinger.*

36. **Quality Meats:** *griots,* the philosopher-poet-historians of West African groups, were revered yet not buried with the rest of the tribe—instead they were left in trees for the buzzards.

37. **Out Getting Ribs:** *for Professor Thomas Sayers Ellis.*

38. **Shadow Boxing: ST JOE LOUIS:** Gentleman Joe pictured in the corner of a room, slight slouch, by photographer Irving Penn would seem to be one inspiration for this painting. The snakes in BSQT's title refer to the Brown Bombers managers and others—for Louis, tho he made millions, in the end welcomed folks to Vegas from a wheelchair & died impoverished. SUGAR RAY: Including "Robinson," none of these are the boxer's "real" names.

39. **B.O.:** In the voice of Andy Warhol. Text from Warhol's *Diaries* & *Philosophy*.

41. **Onion Gum:** To be read up tempo, *al forte.*

46. **Coke® (The Real Thing):** *white girl* is street slang for cocaine.

48. **Self-Portrait as a Heel:** John Belushi, comedian, star of *Saturday Night Live* and *The Blues Brothers*, died of a drug overdose in Los Angeles, 1982. See Bob Woodward's *Wired*.

49. **Self-Portrait as a Heel, Part Two:** Los Angeles was also the scene of comedian/shaman Richard Pryor's accident in which he suffered third-degree burns and almost died after freebasing. Pryor, now suffering from MS, now says it was self-immolation.

53. **Horn Players:** *for Michael S. Harper. Cows* & *lines* are both terms for money, coined by be-boppers. See *Kenyon Review* article.

56. **Revised Undiscovered Genius:** Bill Traylor, former slave, was a self-taught artist who began painting in his old age in Mobile, Alabama.

65. **Zydeco:** A type of music played traditionally with accordions & washboards, originating in southern Louisiana. The name, some believe, comes from a Creole adaptation of *les haricots,* or green beans.

67. **Logo:** The quotes come from a photograph by Dawoud Bey.

72. **Fois Gras:** *for Elizabeth Alexander.* Based on the young man, David Hampton, who pretended to be Sidney Poitier's son to gain access to wealthy New Yorkers. The phrase *beautiful, a mulatto girl…*is taken from Warhol's *Diaries*.

73. **Antar:** *for Nuar Alsadir.* Rousseau refers not to the philosopher, but rather the self-taught artist, Le Douanier, called so by his artist friends (Picasso among them), because he worked at a post office.

75. **Warhol Attends Cohn's Final B-day:** Roy Cohn served under McCarthy & was a rabid anti-communist, helping send the Rosenbergs to the electric chair & blacklisting/destroying many a career. Tho gay himself, he often persecuted others for their sexuality. He was also the lawyer for the owners of Studio 54—who later went on to open the Palladium—while they were under investigation for, and ultimately convicted of, tax evasion. Cohn died of AIDS in 1986.

77. **Peruvian Maid:** *for Danny Rimer.*

79. **Last Supper:** Warhol died from complications after routine gall bladder surgery. In the previous year he had shown a series of Last Supper paintings, silkscreened from a cheap copy of DaVinci's painting. He also executed a number of Last Suppers painted by hand, something Warhol had not done in two decades, but had taken up again in his collaborations with BSQT. These last paintings often include apocalyptic phrases from religious or psuedo-scientific flyers handed out on the street.

87. **Charlie Chan on Horn:** *for John Yau.* Since recording this single, we have learnt that CHAN appears in many a painting; Chan was also the name of Charlie Parker's wife.

89. **Riddle Me This Batman:** *for the late Jerry Badanes*, joke teller and inspiration, who passed away suddenly during the composition of this canto. The Bat represents both a sign of life and of death: Batman always in peril, about to die cliffhanger style; yet always saved, vampiric, nocturnal, death-defying.

90. **Nature Morte:** Found in a painting, KING PLEASURE is a jazz vocalist known for rendering scat & vocal "translations" of jazz tunes.

97. **The Mechanics:** Go see Alfred Hitchcock's *Lifeboat,* and John Singleton Copley's painting *Watson and the Shark.*

102. **Kalik:** The first stanza refers to Henry Dumas, a young poet shot & killed by NYPD in 1968, reportedly for jumping a subway turnstile. Many have linked the shooting to Dumas's radical politics during the time. Marat of course refers to the famous murder & painting; Basquiat features DEATH OF MARAT in a little-seen 1988 painting called *Kalik.*

103. **Eroica:** Leo Malca pointed out to me how the two paintings by this title actually began as one canvas; what is called *Eroica II* originally formed the left side. Latin for 'heroic,' "Eroica" also is the name of Beethoven's 3d Symphony, originally for Napoleon Bonaparte, later for "the memory of a great man." In his research, Kevin Young realized that the definitions listed in the painting most likely came from Clarence Major's groundbreaking *Dictionary of Afro-American Slang,* from 1969.

107. **Two Photographs of Jean-Michel Basquiat:** from a French edition of the work, donated by Professor Ellis.

108. **Pentimento:** The title GRI GRI refers not just to a painting, but to a protective charm in certain hoodoo cultures.

109. **Soul:** *for Elisa Davis.*

110. **The Ninth Circle:** the name of a Village bar bassist-composer Charles Mingus frequented. See the double memoir *Mingus Mingus.*

111. **Epitaph:** AMF is slang for "adios, motherfucker," taken from a painting. In this same early *Untitled* (1981) work, found in the Rubell collection, GREENWOOD & PARA MORIR appears in an uncannily prophetic vision of B's death & burial in Greenwood cemetery seven years later.

112. **Shrine Outside Basquiat's Studio:** If you look closely, you can still see the graffito *Je t'aime Jean-Michel* written on the doorbell.

114. **Relics: THRONE:** Refers to a chair that Basquiat once owned now in the hands of a collector; indeed, it can be seen in the background of a late 1980s photo of the artist. CRAVAT: *for Stephen Frailey,* who sent me the necktie in question. BRAIN©: *CURTIS/LIVE!* at The Bitter End, NYC: Mighty Mighty (Spade and Whitey), I Plan to stay a Believer, We've Only Just Begun, People Get Ready, Stare and Stare, Check out Your Mind, Gypsy Woman, The Makings of You, We the People who are Darker than Blue, (Don't Worry) If There's a Hell Below We're all Going to Go, Stone Junkie. ONE MAN SHOW: The mural of Basquiat, located on Lafayette around the corner from the artist's Great Jones loft, was recently painted over.

116. **Retrospective:** To be read *misterioso.*

Acknowledgments

Singles from this album first aired on the following stations: *Callaloo* ("Jack Johnson" [extended mix], "Hollywood Africans," "Saint Joe Louis Surrounded by Snakes," "Epitaph," "Defacement," "Cassius Clay by Basquiat"); *Crab Orchard Review* ("Rinso," "Soul," & "Stardust"); *DoubleTake* ("Negative"); *Global City Review* ("Toxic"); *Grand Street* ("Onion Gum" & "Savoy"); *Gulf Coast* ("Charlie Chan on Horn"); *Hambone* ("Campbell's Black Bean Soup" & "Poison Oasis"); *Kenyon Review* (EP: Bros. Sausage, "Revised Undiscovered Genius of the Mississippi Delta," "Oleo," "Shrine Outside Basquiat's Studio" & "Riddle Me This Batman"); *The New Yorker* ("Langston Hughes"); *Painted Bride Quarterly* ("Dos Cabezas" & "Oxidation Portrait"); *Pequod* ("Pentimento" [radio edit]); *Ploughshares* ("Satchmo"); and *Ribot* ("Prehistory"). Thanks to the producers and jockeys who gave each airtime.

Other cuts have since appeared on compilations including: *The Beacon Best of 1999* ("Jack Johnson"); *Giant Steps* ("Charlie Chan on Horn" & "Negative"); *The New Generation of American Poets* ("Langston Hughes" & "Campbell's Black Bean Soup"); and *Step into a World* ("Shrine outside Basquiat's Studio").

For help finishing this LP, thanks to a Stegner Fellowship in Poetry, Brown University, University of Georgia, the MacDowell Colony, and the Virginia Center for the Creative Arts. Special thanks to Amy Cappellazzo and Leo Malca, as well as the many curators and gallery spaces, who made possible *Two Cents*, the nationwide exhibit which featured nine of these poems alongside Basquiat's works-on-paper. Thanks to all my faithful readers: there are too many to properly name here, but I hope the dedications found in the Liner Notes, though nowhere complete, help tell something of *Ghosts'* story. I would like to particularly mention Colson Whitehead who believed in *Ghosts* through times when even I didn't.

Thanks go to my agent, Eileen Cope, for her tireless and all too rare support of poetry, as well as Lisa Glover and the rest of the fearless folks at Zoland Books, who made sure *Ghosts* saw the light of day. Lastly, thanks to Gerard Basquiat and the Basquiat Estate for permission to use the images that grace the cover and frontispiece.

These tracks belong to the dead: "Zydeco" is for Da Da who played it; "Mojo" is for Toota who made it.

Recorded in Cambridge, San Francisco, Manhattan, Lynchburg, Providence, and Omicron & Sorosis Studios. Re-mixed at Fisted Pick Productions, Athens, Georgia. No animals harmed in the making.

Index

AMF